INNOVATORS IN DIGITAL NEWS

D1304733

LUCY KÜNG

REUTERS
INSTITUTE for the
STUDY of
JOURNALISM

I.B.TAURIS
LONDON · NEW YORK

Published by I.B.Tauris & Co. Ltd in association with
the Reuters Institute for the Study of Journalism, University of Oxford

Published in 2015 by
I.B.Tauris & Co. Ltd
Reprinted in 2016
London • New York
www.ibtauris.com

Copyright © 2015 Lucy Küng

ISBN: 978 1 78453 416 5
eISBN: 978 0 85773 996 4

A full CIP record for this book is available from the British Library
A full CIP record is available from the Library of Congress

Library of Congress Catalog Card Number: available

Typeset by Riverside Publishing Solutions, Salisbury, SP4 6NQ
Printed and bound by CPI Group (UK) Ltd, Croydon, CR0 4YY

Contents

Executive Summary

The internet and World Wide Web have been part of the media world for well over two decades now. A new landscape of digital media products, platforms, consumption devices, and consumption patterns has emerged, and continues to evolve. These changes have brought challenges for all established media organisations from Hollywood movie studios to public service broadcasters, from the publishers of books and scientific journals to music producers and advertising agencies.

This book focuses on one segment of the many sectors that make up the media industry: digital news organisations. Within that segment it focuses further on just five players: the *Guardian*, the *New York Times*, Quartz, BuzzFeed, and Vice. These players have been chosen because they are all to different degrees and in different ways successful with digital news, even though in the current disrupted and increasingly divergent state of the news industry, the term 'success' can only be used in a qualified way: there are profound differences between digital and analogue revenues, between legacy and clean sheet status, between public ownership, trust ownership, and venture capital backing. So while these are not the only successful actors in the field, they are all recognised to different and disputed extents as leaders, successes, and perhaps role models.

The *Guardian* and the *New York Times* are legacy newspaper organisations that are far along the process of transforming themselves into digital news organisations. Quartz and BuzzFeed are pure player or clean sheet digital news providers. Quartz is 100% news, BuzzFeed is a viral content company that has only moved seriously into news provision in recent years. Vice is a different animal again. News is one element of a broad palette of video content, but its investment in the field is growing, and now equals that of some leading legacy players.

In this book, a series of detailed case studies explores how these five organisations approach digital news, how these activities are anchored in the larger organisation, the corporate strategies and rationales that underlie them, and the cultures, competencies, processes, and measures involved in the implementation of their approaches to digital news.

The book then identifies commonalities in these cases. It pinpoints and discusses shared elements in how they go about their business and characteristics that contribute to their performance. Drawing on this analysis, it highlights precepts, concepts, and approaches which may be of value to other organisations facing similar challenges. It does not provide a 'recipe' for succeeding with digital news, but identifies a set of elements common to all these players that contribute to their success.

Chapter 1 introduces the book, the goals for writing it, the cases in it, the methodology employed, and relevance of its findings. It discusses how 'success' is defined and how the companies profiled meet that criteria. It explores the characteristics of the digital news they provide, and how these are diverging from conceptions of news in the pre-digital era. The triggers for this shift, technological disruption and attendant shifts in consumption behaviour, and the industry disruption that has resulted are then reviewed in terms of how they have created a new and challenging context for news organisations. The chapter closes with a discussion of the research methodology used, the challenges involved in researching a fast-moving sector, and the consequences these have for the relevance and longevity of findings.

Chapter 2 focuses on the *Guardian*. It explores how the UK newspaper became a pioneer of legacy media reinvention and delineates the role of the Scott Trust in defining its innovation path. It discusses how the paper's early start on digital platforms and subsequent consistent experimentation brought valuable insights into how digital news markets operate and the organisational transitions required to succeed in these, as well as helping to address cultural resistance. The core elements of the *Guardian*'s response to new digital platforms are identified and discussed: the decision to make access to the core product free; the search for growth in international markets as well as the UK; the clearly delineated global target market of liberal, intelligent people; the expansion over new platforms, and the strong synergies between these strategic elements; its commitment to serious journalism, and its 'open' strategy of creating permeability between audiences and journalists; and building and monetising its loyal community via membership and events strategies. It also looks at the financial measures accompanying these moves, including divesting non-core assets, a move into native advertising, and downsizing the legacy business.

The subject of Chapter 3 is the *New York Times*. It discusses the organisation's long heritage, national position, and reputation as a beacon for quality journalism. It outlines its ownership and corporate governance arrangements and the implications these have had on its approach to innovation. It documents the institution's early start with digital innovation and the subsequent and consistent initiatives it has introduced, keeping step with industry developments. It reviews the steps taken to restore financial health to the organisation, including maximising print revenues, divesting non-core businesses, and boosting digital income via its successful introduction of a paywall, niche products, and native advertising. The insights provided in the organisation's own study into internal innovation, their Innovation report, are reviewed, particularly the tension this highlighted between the newsroom culture, with its deep commitment to the highest journalistic standards, and the deeper relationship with users and commercial activities necessary in digital news markets.

Chapter 4 explores Quartz, a digital-only, mobile-first provider of digital news for upmarket audiences launched by the Atlantic Media Company. It explains how the concept for Quartz resulted from *The Atlantic*'s goals of disrupting itself, and of creating a new publication that would 'be what *The Economist* would look like if it had launched in 2012'. It explores the extremely coherent elements of the Quartz formula which involve a set of sophisticated choices and trade-offs. These include the decision to go for 'side-door access' from the start (that is, be social-mobile only initially), its target market (the 'smart, young, and bored at work'), writing style (articles either under 500 or over 800 words, headlines that capture the 'nugget' in each story and are designed to go viral), its much admired 'uncluttered aesthetic' with a continuous feed of stories, big visual elements, the 'obsessions' concept that replaces newspapers' typical beat structure, its tech strategy involving responsive design, HTML, and WordPress, and its 'bespoke native' advertising strategy which involves integrating large ads into the story stream which allows it to charge premium rates to premium advertisers.

BuzzFeed is the subject of Chapter 5. It describes how Jonah Peretti founded the organisation in 2006 as a viral content lab and side project to his main role as co-founder of the Huffington Post, and how its focus on investigating and creating viral content left it perfectly positioned to exploit the growth of social and mobile media. The influence of Jonah Peretti on its news ambitions, its technological choices, its business model (growth not profits and native-only), and its long-term strategic orientation are evaluated. This chapter looks at how BuzzFeed is a tech–media hybrid, how data science governs content creation, and how tech industry principles underlie how the organisation is run. It reviews the four core areas of BuzzFeed content: editorial (including 'Buzz' with its focus on listicles and quizzes, lifestyle content; 'distributed' content for platforms such as Instagram and Pinterest); 'creative' which is native advertising content; and 'motion pictures' – video content. It reviews how news content is an increasingly significant element of its editorial content, the increasing amounts BuzzFeed is investing in the field, and the number of classic news journalists of repute joining the organisation.

Chapter 6 looks at Vice Media, the 'Gen Y' media conglomerate with activities spanning both legacy and digital media all over the globe, and which focuses on video content for youth audiences of which an increasingly important element is news. It explores its beginnings as an alternative magazine in Montreal and how its current 'bad-boy' image and culture is an extension of the personality and modus operandi of its founder Shane Smith. It analyses Vice's extensive video activities on new and traditional platforms, explores Vice's growing investment in news, its controversial approach to the field involving 'immersive news' and 'gonzo scoops', and its successes, including an Emmy awarded for its joint venture series with HBO, and its documentary on Islamic State. Vice's business model, encompassing its relationship with commercial partners, its full-service approach to native advertising, and its high levels of investor funding, is discussed.

The final chapter of the book sifts through the detail of the case studies to identify factors common to these organisations that contribute to their success with digital news. It highlights a set of interlinked elements which need to be viewed systemically: their power lies in their combination, in the virtuous circle that is created when all are present and function together.

At the core of these are three interrelated elements which are standard practice for high-performing organisations – a singularity of purpose about the role of the organisation and the 'value' (in management terms) it creates for its users, high calibre leadership from smart individuals who have developed a viable strategic path forward and have credibility with the culture of the organisation, and a clear and unequivocal strategy that sets boundaries, allows prioritisation, and avoids distractions. Then come two elements specific to some to the emerging digital news industry and to the nature of competition and consumption within it. The first is a blending of journalistic, technological, and commercial competencies, involving a deep integration of tech into editorial processes, the presence of digital editorial thinkers, and content creation processes that are response and data driven. Second comes a 'pro-digital culture' that views the digital news arena as an opportunity (albeit a highly competitive field), that is not particularly nostalgic about the old legacy days, and which is open-minded about using the functionalities of digital technology to reinvent quality news. The final two common elements are not easy to acquire or replicate. The first is an early start. The longer a news organisation has been active in the digital field, the more it has learned about how this functions, and the more attuned it is to the pace of the industry and how innovation is best approached. The final element involves autonomy – the ability to innovate and respond as directly as possible to opportunities and threats in the digital news market. This is directly influenced by ownership arrangements (and the priorities of those stakeholders) and by the financial resources available, both elements that a digital news organisation has limited opportunity to influence.

1

Why are Some Digital News Organisations More Successful than Others?

Innovation is a condition for our survival. And the survival of newspapers is completely dependent on our ability to evolve.[1]

We are now two decades into the internet age. A clear cadre of digital news organisations have emerged that are more successful than others, even if 'success' is difficult to define, and the term 'news' is more widely interpreted than traditionalists would like. The basic question guiding the research in this book is whether there is also a set of common elements in how these digital news organisations go about their business. Are there particular shared characteristics that contribute to their above average performance? If yes, what are these?

Cognoscenti in the digital news field, and inside successful organisations, will probably know most of what is in this book already. But many news providers are still struggling with digital, social, and mobile – with cultural blockages, with implanting the necessary tech skills, or with understanding why BuzzFeed or Vice could even be viewed as competitors, or with why a serious news organisation might even contemplate native advertising.

All news organisations are confronting the challenges posed by the internet, digitalisation, new devices for consuming media content, and social media. A common set of organisation responses is making the rounds too: trips to Silicon Valley by the management team, converged newsrooms, digital-first strategies, 'fail early and fast' innovation strategies, social media metrics to measure Facebook 'likes', and so on.

There is much noise in the media about the transition to digital. A basic goal for this project was simply to screen out the noise, look closely at the data, and investigate what is actually happening. Why are some digital news organisations more successful than others? What is the internal state of their organisations? Are there commonalities in how these successful organisations approach their task? Is it possible to distil out of these cases common elements that underlie success in digital news that can be transferred to other organisations?

So the task of this book is pattern recognition. Through a series of case studies of successful digital news organisations it seeks to achieve three objectives. First, it aims to understand how these organisations operate. What makes them successful? How and why did they enter the news field? How do they go about their work? Second, it looks for commonalities and common themes across these cases. Finally it reviews what can be learnt from this analysis, and pinpoints precepts, concepts, and approaches which may be of value to other organisations facing similar challenges.

Five cases – two legacy, three clean sheet

This book focuses on five digital news organisations that are acknowledged successes – bearing in mind that 'success' is a term that is impossible to assign in a definitive way (see discussion below), and that success at one stage of a tech-driven industry transition does not mean success over the long term (Netscape, Nokia, BlackBerry are all salient examples here).

All of the cases in this book are to some extent competing against each other, but apart from that there are few similarities between them. Two – the *Guardian* and the *New York Times* – are legacy newspaper organisations that are far along the process of transforming themselves into digital news organisations. Two – Quartz and BuzzFeed – are pure player or clean sheet digital news providers. Quartz is 100% news, BuzzFeed is a viral content company that has only moved seriously into news provision in recent years. The last case, Vice, is a different animal again. News is one element of a broad palette of video content, but its investment in the field is growing, and now equals that of some leading legacy players.

What is 'success' in digital news?

Most observers would agree that these five digital news organisations belong in the cohort of leaders, but many would also question how successful they are. They would point out that digital revenues at the

Guardian and the *New York Times* are still a long way away from compensating for their loss in print revenues. BuzzFeed's cat videos and listicles can hardly be considered quality journalism. Quartz is a beautiful digital entity, with many admirable aspects, but a niche player. Vice produces excellent news documentaries on important and difficult subjects, but its 'bad boy' content also extends to sex, drugs, and sponsored content. And so it goes on.

These objections are all true to a point. Yet the *Guardian*, the *New York Times*, BuzzFeed, and Vice all have enormous international digital audiences for their news content. Digital advertising revenues, and for the *New York Times* digital subscription revenues, are flowing and in some cases substantial. BuzzFeed and Vice have been successful in attracting investment funding – $96 million for BuzzFeed and $580 million for Vice. Quartz's digital business news site is seen as the apotheosis of smart digital journalism and has overtaken *The Economist* by some measures in the US (although unlike *The Economist* it does not have a paywall). All are recruiting established journalists from legacy organisations, and those legacy journalists seem happy to join them.

And, of course, there are other digital news organisations that are also recognised as successes and that could equally well have been analysed – the *Financial Times*, *The Economist*, the Huffington Post, and Vox are all obvious candidates. The final selection resulted from a process of optimising between a number of constraints, ranging from the project deadline, the availability of good secondary data in English or German (which ruled out Scandinavian candidates), the need to achieve a balance between different types of organisations (legacy, pure player, type of content, type of market, etc.) and challenges in gaining research access. Gaining access was a significant hurdle, and surprisingly time-consuming to jump over (indeed, it consumed over half the time budget for the entire project). In some cases, access was granted, but too late in the process for a case study to be started. In others, access was approved but for varying reasons proved ultimately unfeasible. In all cases I am extremely grateful to the individuals who made time to talk to me.

'If Vice has become a primary news source, then the world is completely fucked!'

Those who have grown up with a traditional concept of what constitutes quality news have problems categorising organisations like BuzzFeed and

3

Vice as news providers.[2] The issue may be that they did not start off as such. Now all have prioritised news, are investing heavily, and are recruiting pedigreed journalists. But this was not part of their original formulae, nor do they define themselves as primarily news organisations. They do not cover all important news issues, nor do they pretend to. Yet they are investing in news journalism, in foreign coverage, and in investigative journalism. Further, they are attracting advertisers, investors, and in the case of Vice and BuzzFeed, the millennial audiences that are lukewarm about the legacy media's digital offerings.

They are also 'reverse entrants' into the news field and this makes them dangerous competitors for long-time news organisations. BuzzFeed and Vice 'discovered' news while focusing on other strategic agendas. In a similar way Amazon upended the book publishing industry, although that was never its core original intention. The industry did however lie in the path of its digital distribution ambitions, and was sideswiped as a result.

Thus this book looks at five digital news organisations that are successful, but the nature of that success differs, and qualifications apply in all cases. Nonetheless, this research seeks to uncover why this group of organisations are successful, however that term is defined.

Context

The main change is that news businesses 1946–2005 were mostly monopolies and oligopolies, and now they're not. Wrenching change for anyone.[3]

The extent of disruption in legacy news is sobering. Long-established organisations have been derailed by a cascading series of interlinked technology-driven changes – starting with the internet, and moving swiftly through tablets, smart phones, and the social media. The number of advertising channels has increased and newspapers' pricing power in ad sales has decreased. In the words of the *New York Times*'s Mark Thompson, they have moved from high-margin to low-margin businesses in a short space of time. They have significant fixed cost bases linked to their historic legacy operations and limited opportunities for reducing these, especially while print revenues are still delivering the bulk of their income.

While this has been very surprising for the sector, theoretically it is not surprising at all. The syndrome by which leading players at one stage in a technology cycle tend to be unseated when disruptive technology ushers in the next has been reported on and investigated by academics stretching back at least to Marx and Schumpeter but more recently by Robert A. Burgelman at Stanford, Michael L. Tushman at the Harvard Business School, and of course Clayton Christensen, author of *The Innovator's Dilemma*.

The news industry is facing a classic case of disruptive innovation. The effect the invention of the internet has had on the print newspaper is similar to the effect the launch of the railways had on horse-drawn transportation. This simile helps because it underlines that while the basic need – the provision of news and information about the world – has remained the same, the technologies used to answer that need are fundamentally different. Newspapers are effectively being asked to change from providers of horse-drawn transportation into railway companies – expressing their challenge in this way underlines the enormous scope of change required, and explains why so few are succeeding in transforming themselves. Shifting from print news to digital news is equivalent to closing the stables, selling the horses, and buying a railway. A different business entirely.

Why case studies?

In terms of innovation in digital news, industry is ahead of theory. Researchers are scrambling to keep abreast of the industry transformation. Organisations are changing permanently. New entrants are emerging. New initiatives are being launched. Leading individuals are changing roles.

This state of affairs dictated the research process used for this book. Such a degree of change predicates an exploratory approach, based around case studies. Cases can provide a narrative explanation of how innovation is being approached and can accommodate ongoing developments, to an extent. They are also accessible. And while a small group of industry followers are *au fait* with these players and the nuances of their stories, many in the industry (including myself before I started this project) are not. Case studies can provide a general introduction and overview, can accommodate differences in individual organisations' situations (important if attempts are to be made to transfer learning), and yet allow common conclusions to be drawn.

About the research

The initial plan was to combine secondary, desk research with primary data from interviews, and to partner secondary data with equivalent amounts of primary data. However, for a range of reasons, this was not feasible. Primary research was more complex than anticipated – a function ironically of the pace in the digital news sector and the heavy workloads of those leading the organisations.

Since the initial goal was to research, write, and deliver in one year (which did not in the end prove possible) the methodology underwent what the tech industry calls a pivot. Complete cases were developed using secondary data, and preliminary conclusions concerning the common factors behind successful digital innovation were developed from these. Primary interviews were then used to check the validity of conclusions and further develop them. To some extent this was a mirror of the product development process being adopted by the organisations under review: release as beta, revise according to feedback. Overall this worked well. The single significant disadvantage was that I could not get deep insights into innovation processes and organisation culture.

An explanatory point is needed for readers concerning displayed quotations in the text. There are two types. Those with an endnote come from secondary sources, and the endnote provides details of what these sources are. Quotes referenced as 'interviewee' come from primary interviews. Since these were given on condition of anonymity, more information cannot be provided. The endmatter of the book, however, provides full details of interviews conducted for the project.

Data on the digital news industry

There are massive amounts of data on digital news media available on the internet. In addition to what features in the 'regular' press, CEOs and key players have keynotes and interviews on YouTube (60+ videos featuring Jonah Peretti for example and at least 20 of Mark Thompson). Institutes such as the Nieman Journalism Lab at Harvard, the American Press Institute, the Poynter Institute, the Pew Research Center, and tech industry specialists such as Gigaom, The Media Briefing, and Monday Note research, analyse, and evaluate digital news developments with great frequency. Reddit and LinkedIn have all kinds of surprising material from individuals in these cases (for example internal strategy memos from Peretti, or Shane Smith podcasts).

Such data do carry disadvantages. The quantity and quality is uneven – BuzzFeed has the most coverage, Vice the least in text form. Further, secondary data cannot be interrogated. It reflects prevailing industry fads and interpretations. It picks up any memes abroad in the industry and is influenced by the views of particularly vocal industry commentators. The risk of confirmation bias is high, and challenging received wisdom is difficult. Those fads can be in turn influenced by the organisations' own corporate communications strategies. Efforts were made to counteract these problems by using as wide a range of sources as possible. Further, findings were fed back not only to interviewees in organisations, but also to a number of industry experts.

Provisos to bear in mind

Before moving on to the cases, some provisos need to be made. First, each of the organisations profiled needs to be understood as a distinct entity. The cases are different. Each news provider has a unique origin, ownership arrangements, history, culture, asset portfolio, editorial emphasis, and so on. The degree of context dependency is significant, and this limits the ability to transfer learning from one case to another.

And a final point: the focus of this book is the digital news organisation itself; the context and content of the innovation taking place, not the news output. Its goal is to document how organisations that produce news are changing as a result of digitalisation and the internet, and how those who are succeeding in a truly difficult environment are managing to achieve that. The wider implications of this innovation for journalism, and for the societal roles of journalism, are not the focus of this book and the cases and discussion in it, although hopefully they can inform and enrich that debate which should, and certainly will, take place.

2

The *Guardian* – 'Global, Open, Digital'

The *Guardian* is a pioneer in legacy reinvention. It has successfully transformed itself from liberal British broadsheet into a leading global provider of digital news in the English language. Its monthly uniques for October 2014 narrowly overtook those of the *New York Times*. It has won accolades for its online activities as well as a Pulitzer Prize for its investigative journalism. 'Digital first' has been a leitmotiv since the turn of the millennium – unofficial at first but then increasingly officially.

This is a perhaps surprising position for a newspaper founded in 1821 by a group of liberal manufacturers in Manchester. Its journey began, as with many legacy media firms' digital transitions, with a CEO visit to Silicon Valley. Alan Rusbridger's visit in 1994 was earlier than most (groups of legacy media leaders from Europe are still making the pilgrimage). Like John Birt, the BBC Director General who went a year later and initiated BBC Online afterwards, Rusbridger returned a digital evangelist. The internet was the future[1] and the *Guardian* needed to transform itself.

Guardian News Media (GNM) revenues for 2014 were £210.2 million.[2] Guardian Media Group (GMG) revenues were £549.2 million, up from £523.3 million the previous year, and reflecting profit on the sale of its stake in Trader Media. Digital revenues were £69.5 million, an increase of 24% on the previous year. Underlying operating losses at GNM were £19.6 million, down from £26.6 million in 2013. At the end of March 2014 its monthly global uniques were 102.3 million, up from 78.3 million in 2013.

Headquartered in London, the *Guardian* has around 1,600 staff worldwide, of which 583 are journalists and 150 work in digital tech, as designers, developers, and engineers. Along with its sister Sunday paper, the *Observer*, it belongs to the Guardian Media Group (GMG), which in turn has a single shareholder, the Scott Trust. The new editor of the *Guardian*, announced while this book was in the midst of the publishing process, is Katharine Viner.

'As heretofore'

> *Each editor is told – this is literally the only instruction – to carry the*
> *Guardian on 'as heretofore'. That means understanding the spirit, culture*
> *and purpose of the paper and interpreting it for the present. All that is*
> *only possible because of the unique Scott Trust, set up in 1936 to ensure*
> *the Guardian survives in perpetuity.*[3]

The Scott Trust has underwritten the newspaper's digital ambitions. To understand the *Guardian*'s digital strategy, it is important to understand the influence of Scott Trust governance on its strategic choices.

The Trust was established in 1936 with a sole responsibility: to safeguard the journalistic freedom and liberal values of the *Guardian* by securing its financial and editorial independence in perpetuity. The *Guardian* must function as a profit-seeking enterprise managed in an efficient and cost-effective way. Profits must be reinvested to 'sustain journalism that is free from commercial or political interference'. In 2008 the Scott Trust became a limited company, but its role and responsibility for protecting the *Guardian* were enshrined in its new constitution.

The Trust appoints the editor of the *Guardian*, who is required to maintain the paper's editorial policy on 'the same lines and in the same spirit as heretofore'. The Trust's policy is not to interfere with the editor's decisions. Alan Rusbridger, editor since 1995 (and also member of the Scott Trust), retired in 2015, and will become Chair of the Scott Trust in 2016.

The Trust sets the tone for the leadership approach and corporate culture. There is a low hierarchy, 'open management' style, and a tradition of broad consultation (a staff ballot is part of the decision-making process for the appointment of the editor). The daily morning conferences which are chaired by the editor and attended by top managers are open to all employees, and are attended by product developers and engineers as well as journalists.[4]

> *The traditions of the Guardian have always been to create a bottom-up*
> *devolved organisation where the editor edits with a very light touch, and*
> *I think that does help cultural innovation. Individuals are much more*
> *empowered to take individual positions and set up little units to do things.*
> *In the early days of the internet, we were on to it much more quickly than*
> *anyone else in this country. We went in ambitiously early on, and we*

weren't waiting on the view of one publisher or proprietor who didn't believe in it or hadn't caught up with it.[5]

The *Guardian*'s culture and governance arrangements mean it must move forward while respecting and keeping continuity with its past. The process by which digital activities moved first to level with print and then to overtake them in strategic importance has required great sensitivity on the part of senior managers. Now, 'print is still much loved' but digital is 'central and primary'.

The *Guardian*'s culture, including an ambivalence towards commercialism rooted in the values of the Scott Trust, complicates organisational change programmes and prescribes their approach:

> *We have a complicating factor which is that this is a unionised place and there is a deep-seated desire to do things consensually and to take them with you [...] some people think that slows things up, quite a lot, and it can slow things up, but I think the net result is a better one for the workforce. (Interviewee)*

> *We've reduced the numbers, but we haven't done it the way others have done it. (Interviewee)*

'Starting early gives you a big audience'

> *The hardest part [...] has been the realisation that you don't automatically get an audience [...] For someone with a print background you are accustomed to the fact that if it makes the editor's cut – gets into the paper – you're going to find an audience [...] It's entirely the other way round as a digital journalist. The realisation that you have to go and find your audience – they're not going to just come and read it – has been transformational.*[6]

The *Guardian* launched theguardian.co.uk in 1999. Its early start means many mistakes, much learning, and a by now substantial knowledge base, as well as market share:

> *We've been through a lot of the growing pains, so whether it comes down to tooling or how we build products or even our audience insights, we've got a better understanding of the things that are important. (Interviewee)*

Starting early also helped to limit cultural resistance, or perhaps, speed the culture shift – in the words of an interviewee, to 'bring individuals along on the journey':

Reporters often exist in peer groups. We were much in the vanguard with open and free, and that could have acted as an individual drag on change, but I think that because of the success of the numbers and the defining nature of the site, we've often been seen at the forefront of change [...] Early successes helped in terms of proving the argument [...] a lot of the journalists that we have are very articulate, very bright, sceptical, and they want an audience for their work, and they recognise that audiences come in many shapes and forms. (Interviewee)

An early architect of digital transformation was Emily Bell, who became Executive Editor of the Media Guardian website in 2000 and Editor-in-Chief of the website (then known as Guardian Unlimited), a year later. In 2006 she was made Director of Digital Content for Guardian News and Media and appointed to the board. This marked the start of a serious transformation into a digital media company:

We have been in a state of permanent revolution since 2005 in some senses, but there's also been an awful lot of continuity, starting with Alan. (Interviewee)

In 2011 a 'digital-first strategy' was announced. This 'major transformation' sought to double digital revenues to nearly £100 million and save £25 million by 2016. To achieve this resources would be shifted from print to digital, and investments would be made in brand marketing. Chief Executive Andrew Miller warned that without tough measures the company could run out of cash in three to five years.

A year later, in 2012, Wolfgang Blau was recruited as Digital Strategy Director from Zeit Online, and tasked with 'helping grow global audiences and revenues by developing new digital platforms that deepen reader engagement and provide new opportunities to commercial parties'.[7] The newspaper's daily editions were also redesigned, away from news and towards analysis, to make it, in Rusbridger's words, 'as relevant at 9pm as 9am'.[8]

By May 2013 theguardian.co.uk was the UK's second biggest national newspaper website, with 4.7 million unique browsers a day worldwide, and

81 million unique browsers and 470 million page views per month. Internationally it was the third most popular English-language newspaper website in the world, behind the *Daily Mail* and the *New York Times*. Indeed, international audiences had grown to the point where the UK represented only a third of the total. A new global domain, 'theguardian.com', was launched to function as a single destination for all digital content, simplify the user experience, and open up commercial opportunities in markets throughout the globe.

In 2014 Janine Gibson was brought back from the *Guardian US* to be Editor-in-Chief of theguardian.com. This move underlines that, while the organisation still 'bears witness' to its print origins, and to the financial contribution made by print, digital is the future, and there is still a long transition journey to be made:

> It is still delivering the lion's share of revenues, so it's critically important for that but if you look at the big macro trends and the move to mobile, the challenges around attention, how we are going to curate globally, the thinking around that isn't print, it isn't the lessons of print. (Interviewee)

Transition tensions

Tanya Cordrey, Chief Digital Officer, has described her role as to ensure that everyone in the organisation is 'putting a digital hat on', and 'feels empowered to do amazing digital things'.[9] Putting a digital hat on to an organisation with a substantial legacy 'head' is trickier than it sounds.

A digital mindset requires sooner or later a digital toolset. New skills are required, skills that are not part of the print journalist toolkit:

> So what skills do you need when you are building stories that are digital from the beginning? You need developers, you need people who can do still images, still are really important, you need multimedia, you need video, you need design.
>
> This is what I mean. Once you start moving towards that digital mindset, all of a sudden, things change. It's not just reporters and editors and photographers and layout people and so I want to build a visuals team here that is ready for that, not just the current thing.

13

The people I would need to do that are almost certainly not in newsrooms. Agencies, maybe working at media companies, but in the tech shop, something like that [...] These are people who need to write code, serious code. (Interviewee)

Increasingly these key individuals are self-taught:

The younger generation of designers are coming up which can build their own stuff. Very, very powerful [...] They are self-taught, they just grew up doing stuff in their bedrooms. It's brilliant when you have that because it speeds up things incredibly. (Interviewee)

Now about 150 digital staff are engaged in product, engineering, data, and analytics. Editorial and technical staff sit together, partly to allow digital culture to permeate the journalistic mindsets, and also to ensure that new digital tools work well for journalists and improve user experience.

'The best digital products are not made out of things that look like a newspaper'

New staff with new skills inevitably create new types of content. The era of repurposing from print to the homepage is waning. It is not easy for a single news organisation to serve both print and digital audiences well:

When you have 80% of your revenues coming from print, you can do some things that matter for the digital audience, but at the end of the day the thing that matters is serving the print audience first. And this is completely in conflict with serving a digital audience. So as a result the digital piece is always going to be the downstream product, the backwater, and so for someone [...] trying to make digital product, it's really, really hard, because everything you want to make you have these pieces and each of them is shaped like a piece of a newspaper [...] the Lego blocks are of the wrong shape, but you can't change that because if you change it they will have to build a second newsroom to build it or you have to stop doing things for print and you have to make a decision that the digital audience is more important than the print audience – really hard to do. (Interviewee)

However, the content components of a print newspaper are increasingly unsuitable for a digital publication, especially when consumption is shifting towards mobile and social:

> *From the product side it is crazy because you are trying to make a product yet all the building blocks you have are shaped like a newspaper, like a traditional 200-year-old newspaper. It's a by-lined article, it's a photo that goes with that article, all the pieces you have to create product are shaped like the legacy thing. And that's why it's tough doing product when editorial is not involved. (Interviewee)*

In addition to a new mindset, new skills, new content formats, there are even subtler differences between print and digital domains:

> *There's something about the rhythm of a newspaper that just – if you've only got one go at it, then you want it to be as good as possible. With digital you can reiterate and change, light and shade, and move things around, and you can look at the traffic, and you can keep doing it, it's sort of continuous. The problem with print is that you have to sort of fix on something ... those two modes of behaviour are in a certain tension. (Interviewee)*

The product team uses agile methodologies and aims at continual development. Developers release code several times each day:

> *You've got to find out it was a bad idea much sooner in the process and that can be quite hard, and I think it's harder for established news operations to grasp than start-ups, where you don't have the brand or you don't have the big audience and you don't have the fears around quality. (Interviewee)*

Nonetheless, it is still a way away from the 'minimum viable design', 'release fast and innovate' tech industry approaches:

> *We have this challenge here to be honest [that can] become quite onerous: 'that's not good enough, that's not good enough'. The audience probably thinks that it is. If we are 90% happy they can be 100% [...] You always set a quality bar around design which is really, really hard. But that can often mean that you can move quite slowly. And you could get things out, learn about them and see if they are working first of all. (Interviewee)*

Free – 'a single bet on the future'

> *To save the Guardian, Rusbridger has pushed to transform it into a global newspaper, aimed at engaged, anti-establishment readers and available entirely for free.*[10]

The *Guardian* has followed a consistent trajectory right from the start: free access to the core online product and go for growth (although it does carry advertising – print and online). This 'single bet on the future'[11] is the defining, central pillar of the *Guardian's* strategy, the point from which other elements radiate. It is also the source of most external criticism, which questions the commercial logic of long-term losses combined with free access.

'Free' is however an almost inevitable choice for the *Guardian*, and the inevitable corollary of two things: first, ownership by the Scott Trust and its public-service-leaning news values, and second, the presence in its home markets of a full-blown public service news organisation with a huge national news audience:

> *If the core purpose of the Scott Trust is to keep the Guardian going in perpetuity, there is no choice [...] The Guardian has only 60,000 subscribers [...] It was competing with the BBC, which has the largest free website in the world. (Interviewee)*

A third 'enabling' factor is that the *Guardian* publishes in English. Free can be sustainable not simply because of the Scott Trust underpinnings, but because of the enormous English-language markets overseas.

'The *Guardian* has been really successful at ... building a global audience, shockingly good'

The scale of traffic required for free to work can only be found by expanding overseas audiences. In the words of CEO Andrew Miller:

> *We need to be global [...] We could not survive in the UK with the 'oversupply' of newspapers and the omnipresence of the BBC.*[12]

Digital-only editions were launched in the US in 2011 and Australia in 2013 and there is talk of Guardian India. Overall, the goal is to become:

a leading global news and media brand, with offices around the world,
and an ever-growing worldwide audience accessing Guardian journalism
every minute of every day.[13]

This strategy is succeeding. In June 2013 the US site attracted 27 million unique visitors, more than the UK version.[14] Monthly global uniques have overtaken the *New York Times* (although that publication has a paywall). International expansion is not only a commercial priority, it meets the journalistic ambitions also.

The sort of journalism we do, we have to have those big ticket numbers,
you have to have enterprise journalism, the stuff that's expected, the
difficult stuff, the investigations. (Interviewee)

'A global community of liberal intelligent people'

The *Guardian* has a clear, differentiated target market and an equally clear sense of the product it will present to them. Rusbridger sought to create 'a global community of liberal intelligent people'[15] and offer them a 'newspaper of protest, an outsider brand [...] with a liberal view of the world'.[16] This audience is youngish, and more likely to be engaged and to become actively involved with the site, contributing content, opinion, or commentary. This goal works for the strategy, for the journalism, and for advertisers, and Rusbridger notes:

With a rigid pay wall, you end up with a small, élite audience, with
restricted access for everyone else. We want a large audience and
international influence, and not just with élites. That appears to be an
attractive mission for advertisers.[17]

'The world's leading liberal voice'

The *Guardian*'s business model is clear (free online), as is its target market (youngish, English-speaking, liberal, digitally connected). A further pillar of its digital strategy, and a central pillar of its culture, is that the *Guardian* sees itself as a 'serious journalistic endeavour',[18] one that will stand up to authority when necessary.

This translates into a serious commitment to investigative journalism, which has combined with its global ambitions and digital platform to produce a series of journalistic scoops that have brought it further international profile. In 2009 it published a series of stories revealing how the *News of the World*, a UK tabloid newspaper owned by Rupert Murdoch, had bribed the police and hacked the phones of celebrities, politicians, and the royal family. The fall-out from this scandal led to the closure of the *News of the World*. In 2010, in collaboration with a number of publications from other countries, it published a series of documents from the Wikileaks website which exposed atrocities committed in Iraq and Afghanistan, and disclosed confidential diplomatic exchanges. In 2013 it published a series of classified documents that showed how the US National Security Agency (NSA) had monitored millions of private emails and phone calls, and disclosed discussions with and about foreign governments. These documents were made available by Edward Snowden, a former NSA contractor. This reporting won the *Guardian* and the *Washington Post* a Pulitzer Prize for Public Service, widely regarded as the most prestigious award in journalism. Its piece, 'Edward Snowden: The Whistleblower behind the NSA Surveillance Revelations', was the most downloaded piece of content for 2013.

Critics observe that the *Guardian* did not manage to increase online advertising sales on the back of this success. It has been suggested that the involvement with Snowden and the NSA leaks did not attract readers but rather damaged the *Guardian*'s image in the US.

'We try to be distinctive through tone'

While the journalistic agenda is serious, the content can be lightweight:

> *There is also a sense of fun and irreverence that we have. The New York Times does serious journalism, and it looks serious. In the Guardian there is light and shade. There are serious issues that we tackle head on, but there is also an irreverence, it doesn't take itself too seriously, but will tackle serious subjects head on fearlessly. That's the mix. (Interviewee)*

This distinguishes it from the *New York Times*:

> *The Guardian is a little more playful about what it publishes [...] it is not a paper of record [...] the definitive, authoritative take [...] and like it or*

not, the New York Times is looked at [...] as the surrogate mouthpiece of the United States. (Interviewee)

The paper's campaigning editorial stance, combined with free online access and a global presence, has brought commercial benefits. Its NSA revelations, for example, were read online by 7 million people on a single day in June 2013. Over the course of the subsequent month, the *Guardian* and *Observer's* combined UK print and online readership was 13.2 million,[19] for CEO Andrew Miller proof that the formula of free × online × quality can work.

'We do things out in the open, we show the workings'

We are putting our commentators in the same space as all our readers and letting them fight it out. That's very challenging for journalists and the paper.[20]

'Open' is another pillar of the *Guardian's* strategy. Open means 'a permeability between the audience and our journalists' in the words of one interviewee, an open, two-way relationship between the organisation and its audiences. It is open to challenge, its processes are as transparent as possible, and readers are encouraged to participate in the journalistic venture.

Open links to serious journalism, to 'global', and also into 'free':

That also kicks into the global nature. If we are opening in America, should we put it behind a paywall? [...] And quite a few things that we have done [...] things that we are very well known for – hacking, World Cup slaves, FGM, Snowden, Wikileaks [...] is based on maximising that audience, otherwise, what are we there for? (Interviewee)

A central element is the 'Comment is Free' concept, launched in 2006. This is an area of the website dedicated to diverse discussion and debate, and open to voices that might otherwise not have access to such a public outlet.

Be at the heart of our communities

Increased participation and engagement is an important goal of 'open'. The *Guardian* wants to position itself at the heart of its core constituencies, to encourage conversations between community members, offering ways for them to share, discover, and disseminate opinions, stories, and data. In addition to inviting comment from users, it is active on Twitter, Facebook, and YouTube and developing what it calls 'professional hubs' of users (with external partners) with similar professional interests. This aspect of its strategy unites commercial and editorial goals. The online environment is transparent, two-way, and increasingly conversational. 'Open' deepens the relationship with its audiences, and builds trust, loyalty, and engagement. Commercially, the greater the reader involvement the bigger the audience, and the higher the digital revenues. As Rusbridger dryly noted during an interview for this book: 'Clients and agencies like open too – it's a very effective money making idea.' Through the *Guardian*, advertisers can access 'conversations'[21] between community members, which is appreciated by advertising agencies, who, according to Business Director, Multimedia and Brand Extensions, Stephen Folwell, recognise that: 'if you can get a message aboard among that community, it will spread.'[22]

Expand over more platforms to feed traffic

If the *Guardian* is to remain free online, then it needs scale. Building international audiences is one element of this strategy. A second is to expand progressively across new media platforms as they emerge. Accordingly it has launched a series of new products and services which, unlike the core website, are generally not free. They include:

- iPad edition available via a paid-for app. This is a reformatted edition of the *Guardian*'s (paid-for) Monday to Saturday newspaper and the *Observer* on Sunday's newspaper, as well as some content from the online site. In 2013, the *Guardian* had 23,000 paying iPad readers.
- Mobile phone apps. Both free and premium apps are available for Android, iPhone, and Blackberry operating systems. In 2013 it had 57,000 paid-for iPhone app users.
- Kindle edition. This offers content from the day's newspaper, including all the editorial sections and supplements.
- Guardian Eyewitness app (free and premium versions).
- Social – Twitter, Facebook, YouTube pages.

- Multiple platforms for content means the *Guardian* has more peak times (noon for the website and apps, mid-afternoon for Facebook, and late evening for iPad and the website). It tailors content to these new peaks, increasing demand for advertising, and thus increasing revenues.[23]

'Get readers to reveal something of themselves, then more over time'

Like many legacy media organisations who have woken up to the competitive threat posed by disrupters like Google and Facebook, registration is a priority. Harnessing the commercial potential of communities requires data about their members. To this end, like the majority of its competitors, the *Guardian* tries to get users to register before they use the free site. The resulting data can be used for analytics and programmatic ad selling (the automated buying, placing, and optimising of media inventory) to increase ad revenues.

> *Registration does two things. Having first-party data about your own users is very valuable. Strategically it's important commercially. In addition to that, on the product side, if we know who you are we can build better products around you.*
>
> *And also, because we know our core readers will access us across three different devices, we are not making the best journey across those devices because we don't know who you are. So if I have read a bunch of stuff on my laptop and then open up my mobile phone later, you shouldn't promote the same running order to me. Synchronising across devices isn't difficult. The challenge is finding the things that will get people to sign in.* (Interviewee)

Slim down to the core and balance the books

> *We can either cut our way out, or we can think, 'What is our future?'*[24]

Although cushioned by the Scott Trust, the *Guardian* is still required to be a 'profit-seeking' (although not profit-making) enterprise and to manage itself in 'an efficient and cost-effective way'. Like its legacy peers, it has found balancing the books in the face of declining print revenues challenging, especially in view of its pension commitments and union agreements.

There has been much criticism of its failure to address its cost base and to settle instead for 'sustainable losses'[25] – despite limited cost-cutting exercises and divestments, losses are not yet under control. The business strategy has three prongs: cutting costs, divesting non-core media assets, and developing new revenue streams (native advertising, events, and a membership programme).

CEO Miller does not expect the paper to be profitable in the near future, and in 2014 *The Economist* calculated that profits from the sale of its remaining stake in *Auto Trader* for £650 million in 2014 will only support its current levels of losses for 30 years, and pointed out that this does not constitute ensuring the paper's survival in perpetuity, as mandated by the Scott Trust terms.[26]

Echoing similar moves at the *New York Times*, all non-core media assets have been sold, including the *Manchester Evening News*, radio stations, a property services group, and its remaining stake in the Trader Media Group.

Downsizing the legacy organisation

Cost-cutting is not an obvious cultural fit for the newspaper that has an unofficial tradition of avoiding compulsory redundancies. However, between 2011 and 2012 the newspaper cut around 200 jobs in editorial and commercial divisions. In 2012 it announced it was looking at compulsory redundancies after a voluntary redundancy scheme that sought to reduce the headcount by between 70 and 100 attracted only 30 journalists.[27] In 2013 the editor-in-chief took a £116,000 cut in his total financial package and CEO Andrew Miller waived half of his £202,000 bonus. In February 2013 GMG concluded negotiations aimed at cutting 100 editorial staff as part of plans to take £7 million out of the editorial budget. This included 58 staff (equivalent to 50 full-time positions) taking voluntary redundancy from a total of 650 journalists.

Native advertising and Guardian Labs

Native advertising is a newish priority. As with the *New York Times*, the initiative has been greeted with scepticism, and there is a degree of cognitive dissonance between the concept and the commitment to investigative journalism. In 2013 Guardian Labs was created, a branded content agency 'to work with companies to create marketing campaigns that go beyond buying advertising space online or in the newspaper'. This was launched formally as a division in 2014, with 133 staff including designers, video producers, writers, and strategists. They work with editorial, marketing and digital development teams to develop interactive and cross-media content and live events for clients. In 2014 a deal worth over £1 million was signed with Unilever to create a platform on sustainability that combined interactive, cross-media content and live events.[28]

Guardian Space, Guardian Live, Guardian Membership

> *The Guardian is easy to mock for its sandal-wearing earnestness, its champagne socialism and congenital weakness for typos, but its readers en masse seemed like the kind any editor would be glad to have: curious, questioning, quick to laugh. Seeing the rapport between them and their paper [...] you could easily have assumed that everything in the Guardian was rosy.*[29]

In an interesting move, at the close of 2014 the *Guardian* announced a new initiative that would effectively monetise the tremendous reader loyalty the publication enjoys:

> *Most readers said they would happily contribute money to the 'cause' of the Guardian – but an overwhelming majority also wanted the journalism to be free, so that it could reach the maximum possible audience. A fair number were happy to be subscribers, but the most hands shot up when asked if they would like to be 'members'.*[30]

In 2014, the *Guardian* launched Guardian Space, Guardian Live, and Guardian Membership. These aim to monetise its free-content audience.

> *Membership is a big piece of [revenue generation]. It's different to registration because we are asking you to consider yourself, in some cases we are asking you to pay money, and in other cases we are asking you to commit to being 'on our team'. (Interviewee)*

Guardian Space is a convention centre/conference venue for live events that will launch in 2016, converted from a Grade II-listed Midland Railway goods shed in King's Cross acquired in 2014.

Guardian Live will involve hundreds of events, activities, and courses each week throughout Britain, held in partnership with various educational and cultural organisations. Currently employing around ten people, there are plans to increase the staff from 30 to 50 in the UK, and then expand into the US and Australia in 2015.

Guardian Membership is a new membership model that aims to deepen the relationship with readers, as well as generate revenues. The rationale is that the better it knows its readers, the greater the relevance of its content, and the greater the value of that content for those readers. There are three membership levels:

- friends, who get access to all the paper's online content and can buy tickets to Guardian Live events;
- partners, who pay £15 a month and get discounted tickets for events, can book in advance and watch livestreams of events;
- patrons will pay £60 a month and can get special access to private events and 'unique experiences' not open to other members.

Other commercial activities

In addition to these relatively recent initiatives, the *Guardian* has a wide range of other longer standing, Jeff Bezos-style initiatives that seek to monetise both hitherto internal aspects of its operations and reader relationships. At a distance these appear more like opportunistic revenue-generating 'patches' than alternations to the core business model, and include the following:

- Professional services. These are B2B products and services that monetise 'back' stages of value chain. The Guardian Digital Agency offers data visualisation, site design, interactive development, and content strategy for desktop and mobile platforms, as well as for print.
- E-commerce. These activities range from reader offers (selling white label products on its website), to holidays offered in conjunction with third parties (Guardian Escapes, a membership-based travel club, and

Guardian Cottages and Villas), and financial products and services (Guardian Moneydeals).

- Networks and partnerships. The *Guardian* has a set of networks ('hubs') focused on specific communities with different degrees of commercialisation. There are hubs addressing professionals in media, education, healthcare, social care, and so on. The Guardian Development Network, which covers development issues, is supported by the Bill and Melinda Gates Foundation. New content concepts are also being developed in partnership with third parties, for example a 'citizen journalism' platform, Guardian Witness, developed in partnership with mobile phone operator, Everything Everywhere. Guardian Cities, a new website section looking at the future of cities around the world, is financially supported by the Rockefeller Foundation.

Decoded

There have been investments as well as divestments. In February 2014 the Guardian Media Group acquired a 15% stake in Decoded, a digital training company that teaches how to 'code in a day'. This was their first digital investment in nearly five years. The organisations hope to benefit from a growing demand for coding skills. Joint activities are anticipated in editorial initiatives, events held via the newspaper's membership programme, launched in 2014.[31]

An early digital mover that kept its momentum

To understand the *Guardian*'s innovation strategy one needs to understand its culture. And to understand the *Guardian*'s culture one needs to understand the Scott Trust. The Trust is the bedrock of the *Guardian*'s culture and has, indirectly perhaps, prescribed many key dimensions of its innovation path: free access, serious journalism, 'openness', membership initiatives, and 'sensitive' downsizing.

The culture and aims of the *Guardian*, founded in 1841, are surprisingly compatible with the emerging global digital ecosystem. A commitment to journalism that 'makes a difference' and an investigative, if not campaigning, stance can be realised even more effectively with the amplification that comes from being a player on a global stage. 'Open' and participatory is perfect positioning in an era where communication is increasingly dominated by social networking. Liberal progressive values are arguably more compatible with the culture of the digital native and digital disrupters in general than the more establishment cultural orientation of other heritage print media organisations.

This could explain why, although there has been cultural resistance to innovation, the *Guardian*'s transition efforts have been far less hobbled by culture than those at other heritage newspapers have been. While 'the moral authority still sits within the newspaper' (interviewee), many in the organisation do see the opportunity in digital, and understand the importance of technology in realising that opportunity.

The *Guardian* was an early digital mover and then managed to keep its momentum; a 'triumph of old-school reporting has been accompanied by spectacular success in new media'.[32] This feat is not to be underestimated, as early movers can easily become early followers. It was lucky in having a strong cadre of senior managers who understood the strategic importance of digital and had the stamina to push their vision. It had a penchant for big bold strategic moves, necessary in disrupted environments, and also not to be underestimated, these moves have been broadly successful. Success, beating the competition, can dissolve cultural opposition very effectively. Perhaps most significantly for the future, its early start and success mean it is now attuned to the pace of the industry and perceives the scale of threat it faces from new competitors. These are all excellent preconditions for future success, but as a legacy player it is nonetheless handicapped by having to run the old while building the new, and the increasing disconnect between the two.

3

The *New York Times* – Digitising 'The Grey Lady'

The New York Times knows about one thing [...] serious journalism [...] That is the point of the New York Times [...] All of the hedgehog's creativity happens within and around that single big idea. And so its choices are inevitably more limited. But the hedgehog never for a moment loses sight of what it is and what it stands for, and nor do its customers. In the incredibly fragmented, crowded world of digital news, that, too, turns out to be a critical advantage, and in the case of the New York Times we hope a winning advantage.[1]

Headquartered in New York, the *New York Times* is a venerable US institution and a byword for quality journalism. It has won 112 Pulitzer Prizes, more than any other news organisation. Founded in 1851, today it is the third largest newspaper in the US by circulation, behind the *Wall Street Journal* and *USA Today*.

The New York Times Company went public in the 1960s, but complicated voting arrangements (Class A shares have only limited voting rights, and the Sulzberger family owns 88% of the Class B shares which have greater voting rights) mean that the controlling interest is held by the Ochs Sulzberger family.

Its annual operating profit for 2014 was $92 million, down from $156 million in 2013, with the fall attributed to investments in digital journalism and severance payments.[2] Revenues were flat, but growth in digital advertising and circulation offset declines in print. Online advertising increased 19.3% on the previous year, primarily driven by its native advertising product, the Paid Posts.[3] At the close of 2014 it had 910,000 paid digital subscribers, a 20% increase on 2013, and it expected to reach the 1 million subscriber milestone in 2015. Digital subscription revenues grew by 13.6% to $44.4 million. With 1,230 journalists the *Times* has the largest news staff of the organisations profiled in this book. In addition it has around 630 digital technologists, working in analytics, design, product, engineering, and R&D.

Modernising a 'beacon of quality journalism'

Nationally and internationally the *Times* stands for excellence in writing, serious journalism, and serious investment in journalism. Its essence is captured in its nickname 'The Grey Lady'. After nearly 20 years of digital innovation this label irritates some inside the organisation, but it captures the publication's national stature and the respect it commands. Similarly the masthead motto, 'All the news that's fit to print', has long been overtaken by the realities of a digital firehose of news (and in 2008 was updated for the website to 'all the news that's fit to click'), but bears witness to the historic ambitions of the paper.

Mark Thompson, President and CEO, joined in November 2012. As CEO he is responsible for strategy, operations, and business units, and required to work closely with the chairman on the vision of the company. On joining he gave growth initiatives in mobile, advertising, video, and global expansion as priorities.

The *Times*'s chairman and publisher is Arthur Ochs Sulzberger Jr, a member of the family that has controlled the New York Times Company for five generations. A peculiarity of the *Times*'s governance structure is that the role of president is sandwiched between that of the chairman and publisher: so Thompson as CEO reports to the chairman Arthur Ochs Sulzberger Jr, but Sulzberger, as publisher, also reports to Thompson. The New York Times Company is both listed on the stock exchange and a family business, with the result that Thompson sits within an unusually complex governance and stakeholder structure.

The appointment of Thompson as CEO of one of the most legacy-heavy US media organisations – a Brit from a public service broadcasting background – was surprising. But his experience of broadcasting and track record in modernising the BBC, also a large, prestigious but traditional organisation,[4] was decisive for Ochs Sulzberger Jr, who had run a lengthy search process:

> We have people who understand print very well, the best in the business [...] We have people who understand advertising well, the best in the business. But our future is on to video, to social, to mobile.[5]

'The digital effort is ... going to be the heart of the organisation'

One of the ways that we want to change the story about the Times, to compete effectively with our new competitors in the digital space, is through innovation. Innovation in areas like digital advertising, but also innovation in content. And we think the opportunities to innovate around very rich media content are great for us.[6]

Thompson inherited an organisation that had already taken huge strides in its transition journey. The *Times* had made an early start with digital and from then on responded speedily to successive waves of industry innovation. A website was launched in 1996. It has had a continuous news desk since 2000. It started to merge print and online in 2005.[7] It created the 'Times Reader', an e-reader app free for subscribers and $15/month for non-subscribers, in 2006. In 2007 it established an Interactive News Technology Team of developer-journalists, led by Aron Pilhofer and Matt Ericson. In 2008 it launched the 'Times Extra', a site that aggregated coverage from other online news sources (discontinued the following year), gave access to its numerous APIs to developers,[8] and opened its archive of 2.8 million articles dating back to 1981, allowing external data journalists to develop visualisations of its data. It launched iPhone and iPod Touch apps in 2008 and an iPad app in 2010, and in the same year it launched TimesCast, a daily video service.

These projects were not all successful (as has been the case for all legacy organisations transitioning to digital news) but, as with the *Guardian*, an early start created competitive advantage, building digital expertise, knowledge of digital markets, and bringing exposure to the organisational challenges of transition.

'The Upshot', machine learning, and a new video strategy

Recent significant innovations have been focused on younger, digital, and mobile audiences. The Upshot (launched 2014) is a politics and policy 'explainer' website that combines data and journalism to help readers 'get to the essence of issues and understand them in a contextual and conversational way'.[9] Run as a semi-autonomous unit, it was set up to fill the gap created by the departure of Nate Silver and his FiveThirtyEight site to ESPN.

By 2014 a machine learning team had been created that combined data engineers, business analysts, and data visualisers to interpret online user data to generate insights into usage and ideas for new products (similar to the algorithm-creation that underlines the recommendation engines on Netflix or Amazon).

Video, viewed as a means of reaching younger audiences, is a priority – as it is for most of the organisations profiled here. A Video Hub was launched in 2014 and now employs around 60 people (of whom 50 work in production and the rest on the commercial side).[10] Short-form video is offered in 14 thematic verticals ranging from health to politics. The content is produced by an in-house team and external partners. Videos are also increasingly added to relevant articles on the website, and included as stand-alone pieces, sometimes functioning as a precursor to a subsequent print story. In addition there is a channel on YouTube and a network of distribution partners including AOL, Yahoo, and MSN. Video access is free and there are no plans for a video paywall. Commercial revenues are generated through pre-roll and sponsorship.[11]

Restoring financial viability

> *Jonah Peretti [...] said in a recent interview that the biggest question for the Times is not how to improve its digital offerings but 'why do they need to have so much revenue?' [...] It's because their cost structure is made for print [...] the challenge that they're facing moving forward is how do they move into a post-print world?*[12]

One of the current ironies for legacy players is that, after decades of solid and assured finances and cash flows, they now suffer from sickly finances and insufficient funding to finance digital innovation and expansion to the extent they would like, certainly in comparison with new players such as BuzzFeed, Vice, and Facebook with whom they must compete for audiences.

The *New York Times* is publicly quoted, and therefore subject to the pressure of quarterly reporting. It does not belong to a non-profit trust like the *Guardian,* which has provided a solid financial cushion to tide it over the digital divide. It does not have the cash runway supplied by a billionaire owner like John Henry at *The Boston Globe* (to whom it sold the paper) or Jeff Bezos at the *Washington Post* (who in addition to 'runway' brings industry-leading competencies in digital technology and in building relationships with digital customers).

The *Times*'s finances were notably precarious in January 2009 after the 2008 collapse of the credit markets. It raised $225 million through a sale and leaseback of its headquarters, but was also forced to grant Mexican telecom mogul Carlos Slim Helú purchase warrants for 15.9 million shares of stock, allowing it to borrow $250 million at an extraordinary interest rate of 14%.

The *Times* repaid Slim in 2011. Slim exercised his purchase warrants in January 2015, acquiring his 15.9 million shares in the company and making him the largest investor. He now holds 16.8% of the Class A shares, but these carry only limited voting rights.[13] The Ochs Sulzberger family are still in control.

In addition, the *Times* has divested non-core assets – the regional papers in 2011, its remaining stake in the Boston Red Sox in 2012, About.com in 2012 and the *Boston Globe* in 2013, in order to focus on the core property, the *New York Times*.

Print revenues – 'declining and volatile'

Today, the print business, while still 'keeping the lights on', is declining and 'volatile', to cite Mark Thompson, as advertising moves 'profoundly (but haphazardly) from print to digital, along with readers'.[14] A central tenet of the *Times*'s print strategy is to retain its loyal print readers and maximise revenues from this group as far as possible, and there have been consistent increases in the news-stand and home delivery prices.

Falling print revenues and only modestly advancing digital ones mean that, despite the success of its paywall which should reach a million subscribers in 2015, and although it is doing better than most of its peers, the *Times* needs to trim activities. While there has been limited expansion in print – the *New York Times Magazine* was relaunched under a new editor – the general picture is one of legacy curtailment.

Overall expenses have been reduced by 2.1%.[15] In June 2014 it was announced that half of the paper's blogs would be gradually shut down or absorbed, although blog-style content would still appear on the website. In October 2014, the Sunday Automobile section was cut (regional sections had been eliminated in 2009, and the Metro combined with the A section in 2008), and the NYT Opinion App which had been launched the previous June was shut down, having failed to find a viable audience.[16] More dramatically, 100 newsroom jobs were cut. Eighty-five staff took buy-out packages and the remainder were laid off, costing $21 million in severance payments.

Accelerating digital revenues

The *Times* is aiming for multiple streams of digital revenues – from a metred paywall, from subscriptions for niche products, and from online advertising, where increasing emphasis is being placed on paid content and sponsorship. In 2012 Arthur Ochs Sulzberger Jr announced a digital growth strategy, 'Invest in the Core', which aimed to accelerate the *Times*'s transition and increase its digital revenues through increased investments in mobile, video, social engagement, and new global markets.

A decisive and defining step in this strategy had been taken the year before when a metred paywall was introduced, followed by a digital subscription plan in March 2012. This move was later described by Thompson as 'the most important and most successful business decision made by the *New York Times* in many years'.[17] Although the paywall generated revenues, more digital reader revenue needed to be raised. New subscription options as well as new products that repackage content for different consumer groups were launched.

In 2013 three new niche subscription products were announced for launch in 2014, the 'biggest initiative since the January 2011 launch of the metered pay system itself'.[18]

- The first was *Food and Dining*, which expanded the dining section of the newspaper with video and how-to features.
- The second was *Need to Know*, which offers a briefing on current events for smartphone, tablet, and web, including aggregated and curated content from third-party sites.
- The third product, *Opinion*, was an op-ed site with similarities to the *Guardian*'s Comment is Free section (this failed to find a market and was closed in 2014).

More niche paid products were added the following year:

- *NYT Now* is a low-cost app for iPhone that combines a subset of *NYT* articles with a curated selection of external content, and morning and evening briefings of key news events. Ten editors curate the content, some of which is available for free. This was designed for mobile and social but resonated also with older consumers who were attracted by the cheaper access to the website it provided (in April 2015 it was suggested that the *NYT* is about to change this into a free, ad-supported product in an attempt to attract more users who may later upgrade to digital subscription plans).
- *Times Premier* gives loyal users 'an enhanced offering that takes you beyond the news, with access to exclusive behind-the-scenes content and expanded benefits only available to *New York Times* subscribers'. It also provides a compilation of articles from the *Times's* archives, and more crossword puzzles.
- A cooking app, which by the end of 2014 had over 8 million users and had been downloaded over 300,000 times (and may come to serve as a template for other niche products[19]).

Global ambitions

We now believe there are compelling possibilities in growing our international audience. We are trying to decide which markets to jump into first, and how to go about doing it.[20]

A less prominent element of the *Times's* strategy is international expansion. The *International Herald Tribune* was rebranded as the *International New York Times* in 2013. In late 2014 the company announced a desire to expand its presence in non-English-speaking markets, and a project was launched to explore foreign-language activities. In the same year it launched a new 'digital hub' in London with 100 staff, to act as a centre for its international offices.

'Riding the wave of content marketing'

The Innovation report noted that by 2013 digital subscriptions were bringing in 35 times the revenues of digital advertising.[21] By mid-2014 digital advertising still only accounted for under 3% of the *Times's* digital revenues.[22] In response, the *Times* like many of its peers introduced native advertising, a decision greeted critically by some in its newsroom and beyond.[23]

Meredith Kopit Levien was appointed in July 2013 as EVP of advertising. Under the motto of 'talent, culture, ad products' she recruited 80 new staff, many with digital skills (an equivalent number left), and encouraged more innovation and creativity in the overall team (around 240).[24] Her major initiative was the 'Paid Posts' native advertising programme, launched in January 2014.[25] The first native adverts, for Dell, were relatively low-key, but subsequent campaigns have sought to match the 'gold standard' of the *Times*'s editorial content. Under the philosophy of 'if you want to make this work, you have got to compete with editorial', a separate in-house content team, the T Brand Studio, under the direction of Adam Aston, a former *BusinessWeek* editor, creates the brand content, much of which is aimed at the luxury segment. It has over 20 staff, including designers, technologists, content strategists, and social media experts, and has produced nearly 40 campaigns.[26]

The *Times*'s native advertising, like that of BuzzFeed and Vice, echoes the culture and character of non-commercial content. Creative standards are extremely high and execution meticulous. 'Women Inmates: Why the Male Model Doesn't Work', a narrative article on failures in the female prison system, was produced to promote the second series of Netflix's *Orange is the New Black*. The series is never directly mentioned, only the author of the memoirs the show is based on.[27] The text is based on extensive research and is synchronised with infographics, video, and audio. 'Grit and Grace' is an essay and set of short videos about three New York City ballet dancers for Cole Haan that combines reporting, video, photography, and illustration and was the first paid post to feature full-bled images.[28]

Native advertising led to a 16.5% increase in digital ad revenue in the third quarter of 2014. The current priority is to expand native advertising on mobile,[29] echoing a shift towards mobile in the preferences of brands and ad agencies. Over half of the *Times*'s digital traffic in the third quarter of 2014 came via mobile devices, but mobile advertising revenues were only 10% of total digital ad revenues.

The Innovation report

Until 2014 the *New York Times* was widely viewed as a poster child for digital transition, 'one of the few traditional media to have successfully morphed into a spectacular digital machine',[30] with 'a gold star for managing the digital transition'.[31] Its status as digital innovator was damaged in May 2014 when an internal document, the 'Innovation' report[32] – a 'deep-dive reporting project on our own paper and industry' – was leaked. It laid bare the challenges facing the organisation and the weaknesses undermining its digital performance.

The depth of analysis this document contains was a boon for this book, but in many ways unfair to the *New York Times*, since nothing comparable was available for the other cases reviewed here. Further, the analysis and attention the report attracted allowed a far more informed analysis of the *New York Times's* innovation path by the industry press than has been possible for the other companies featured.

Key recommendations in the 'Innovation' report

The report originated in a project commissioned by Abramson and led by Arthur Gregg Sulzberger (son of Arthur Ochs Sulzberger) that sought to identify new digital products. Gradually the team's remit expanded into a report analysing the digital challenges facing the organisation. The result is honest, reflective – and sobering. As Frederic Filloux pointed out 'we rarely, if ever, see an internal analysis expressed in such bold terms'.[33]

While praising the *Times's* innovation efforts (including the website redesign, the launch of native advertising, the success of its new apps), the Innovation report analyses the extent of the competition it is facing in digital news. Traffic to the homepage was suffering from the increasing advance of competitors like BuzzFeed, the Huffington Post, and Yahoo News. While 37% of users still came to the site directly, a significant and growing proportion were accessing its online news via search engines and social networks (a problem termed 'the death of the homepage'). It noted the defection of high-profile legacy journalists to digital start-ups and digital-first initiatives from legacy competitors, and the expansion of news activities by new news organisations such as Vice, BuzzFeed, and Vox.

The report made some central recommendations to counter these threats:

- Develop audiences. The *Times* needed to understand its audiences better, build stronger relationships with them, and promote its digital content better (termed 'embracing the reader experience'). A new role was needed that focused on audience development and improved how journalism is packaged and distributed (better tagging and structuring), promotion, and creating a two-way relationship with readers to deepen loyalty. This role would be based in the newsroom but collaborate with the business side.

- Improve collaboration between the newsroom and business side of the organisation (design, technology, consumer insight, R&D, and product staff had far too little contact with the newsroom). It described this change as potentially transformational for the *Times*, and also noted such cooperation was standard practice for many of its competitors. David Leonhardt described how when creating The Upshot he lacked contact with experts on competition, audience, platform strategies, promotion, and user-testing. (Notably, however, the report ducks recommending wholesale integration – also standard for many competitors. Rather, a new management edict would be enough: 'we do believe simply issuing a new policy [...] would send a powerful new signal and unlock a huge store of creative energy and insights'.[34])

- Create a small newsroom strategy team. This would track the external environment (competitors' strategies, changing technology, shifting reader behaviour) and internal projects, and ensure new areas were being followed.

- Map a strategy to make the newsroom a truly digital-first organisation. While the 'health and profitability of our print paper' means the *NYT* does not yet need to be 'aggressively reorganised around a digital-first rather than a print-first schedule', the *Times*, nonetheless, must start 'imagining the newsroom of the future [...] reassessing everything from our roster of talent to our organisational structure to what we do and how we do it'.[35]

Homage to the masthead

Of the 32 people on the Times's masthead [...] four are dead and none of the titles include the words 'software', 'engineering', 'design' or 'technology' [...] But most revealing of all is the choice of language in the 97-page report. The word 'software' does not make a single appearance in the body of the report and it is not until page 63 that the word 'code' makes its debut. It's also clear that the authors could not summon up the courage to stop referring to their audience as 'readers' and begin to call them 'users'.[36]

Perhaps the biggest threat to innovation identified in the report was the newsroom culture. References to its ability to resist and subvert change abound. The newsroom was found to be perfectionist, cautious, and risk averse. It viewed new ideas 'through the lens of worst-case scenarios' and had a tradition of reacting 'defensively by watering down or blocking changes, prompting a phrase that echoes almost daily around the business side: "The newsroom would never allow that"'.[37] It needed to cease believing itself superior to commercial areas, and drop its metaphors 'The Wall' and 'Church and State'.

A great place for journalists, less so for digital talent

The report paints a picture of a masthead-dominated organisation – a marvellous place for journalists, but not for the technologists trying to achieve a digital transition. It warns that while the *Times* needs a 'deeper and broader range of digital talents', it risks 'becoming known as a place that does not fully understand, reward and celebrate digital skills'.[38] Leadership positions need to be open to the digitally talented as well as to journalists.

The report notes that 'our storied brand is less of a draw among digital natives'. The *Times* had not fully grasped that:

> digital talent is in high demand. To hire digital talent will take more money, more persuasion and more freedom once they are within the Times – even when candidates might strike us as young or less accomplished.[39]

The report team interviewed some 'digital departures' to find out why they had left. The answer was they felt their work was not valued or appreciated by leaders, and they felt stifled by tradition and bureaucracy. None regretted leaving.

> The reason producers, platform editors, and developers feel dissatisfied is that they want to play creative roles, not service roles that involve administering and fixing. It would be like reporters coming here hoping to write features but instead we ask them to spend their days editing wire stories into briefs.[40]

'Change in the *New York Times* is like a 30-year marathon'[41]

The *New York Times* moved fast to act on the report findings. Dean Baquet, the new editor-in-chief, created a new tier of newsroom leadership. Four existing deputy executive editors were elevated to this top tier, and additional equally weighted new posts were also created. A new role of Senior Editor for Strategy, who should 'help make sure the report's proposals become reality', went to the report's lead author, Arthur Gregg Sulzberger, whose job, reporting to Baquet, is to:

> *aggressively search for the trends and developments in the industry – from the way people read us as they bounce from mobile to print, to the most Timesian way of finding and grooming a new and bigger audience.*[42]

Kinsey Wilson was recruited from NPR to become Editor for Innovation and Strategy and focus on expanding the mobile apps and serve as the main digital liaison point between the newsroom and the business side. A. G. Sulzberger will focus on specific strategy issues in the newsroom but perhaps only in the mid-term since he is also being groomed for future company leadership.[43]

In August 2014, Alex MacCullum was appointed Assistant Managing Editor for Audience Engagement. This position focuses on interaction and collaboration between the newsroom and business side, using audience analytics to identify target audience segments, and improve reader experience and product. The new audience development department has been successful in implementing measures to improve liaison with the newsroom: 'there was a natural desire for them to happen', according to one of the report's authors.[44] However, the new area required sensitive selling culturally, as evidenced in Dean Baquet's New Year note to the newsroom staff: 'its purpose is not to chase clicks but to expose as many people as possible to our finest work, and to connect us to readers in new and deeper ways.'[45]

Alex MacCullum stressed that this new activity is simply allowing the *Times* to fulfil its traditional role better:

> *The whole mission of BuzzFeed is to get people to share. That is not the mission of the New York Times. The mission of the New York Times is*

about the best journalism in the world and giving people accurate, timely
information. I don't think that BuzzFeed is competing in that space.[46]

A 'digital first' strategy was launched in February 2015 when Dean Baquet
changed the daily 'Page One Meetings' to focus not on what would appear
on page 1 of the paper, but on which stories deserve the best position on
the website, a shift intended to:

Ensure that our digital platforms are much less tethered to print deadlines
give [... and] us more flexibility in targeting readers on mobile [...] and
on platforms like Facebook.[47]

Highly and consistently innovative, but constrained by culture

The *Times* has been extremely successful with digital news, but if its own
Innovation report is to be believed, it has been successful despite its
prowess, standing, reputation, and infrastructure, rather than because of
it. The report provides striking insights into the hurdles a legacy culture, a
culture of journalistic excellence, can erect for innovation. The paper's
own public editor points out, 'Part of the challenge is that print is in the
blood of most of the journalists at the paper.'[48] The tenacity of digital
resistance is surprising and once again underlines the organisational might
of corporate culture.

This is a deeply intelligent, intellectual, connected, and reflective
organisation. It was a very early digital mover. It has successfully introduced
a paywall that is working. It has been lauded industry-wide for initiatives
like The Upshot. It has even mastered the art of the quiz and listicle (its
most visited content of 2013 was 'How Y'all, Youse and You Guys Talk', a
quiz on how your dialect shows your US origins, that was only posted on
the site during the last month of 2013). Yet adjusting the internal balance
between 'digital tech creatives' and journalist creatives is a slow process.

Its future will depend on its ability to change. It does not have deep
pockets and it does have shareholders. However, a viable digital business
model is gaining traction – subscription plus native advertising –
although building these revenues will be an ongoing challenge. But the
most significant challenge will be navigating the cleft between traditional
print and new digital. This is an internal challenge with two dimensions.

The first, stressed again and again in the Innovation report, is getting the newsroom to acknowledge the ascendency of digital technology, to recognise its value and to learn to work with it. The second, also a recurring theme in the Innovation report, is reshaping the relationship between church and state, recognising that a strong independent journalistic voice is not threatened by collaboration with those trying to grow and monetise audiences.

But there is an external dimension also. As it moves forward on its digital path, the *Times* will need to balance feeding the interests of its traditionalist readers, who are sustaining the engine, with those of younger digital audiences, who should become the core of future audiences but may find the traditional 'pedigreed' news tone heavy going in comparison to the other digital news they are consuming.

4

Quartz – What Would *The Economist* Look Like if it had Been Born in 2012?

Social and mobile accounted for the entirety of our strategy at launch [...] We wanted to create a site that would work on all devices [...] and we wanted to build an audience as quickly as possible and it was clear the only way to do that would be on the back of social distribution, so we anticipated that that would be the bulk of our traffic and in fact it has been. 60% of Quartz's audience on any given day is coming through social media.[1]

Quartz is a digital-only provider of global news with a focus on business and aimed at 'influentials' – affluent mobile business people with many digital devices and a penchant for well-written news. According to Kevin J. Delaney, Editor-in-Chief and Co-President, a guiding inspiration was to create a 2012 version of *The Economist*.[2]

Delaney had previously been Managing Editor of WSJ.com, and prior to that a reporter at the *Wall Street Journal*, where he had covered digital players like Google, Twitter, and Facebook. He now leads Quartz in collaboration with Jay Lauf, Publisher and Co-President, who joined Quartz from its parent, *The Atlantic*. Both Delaney and Lauf have been with Quartz since its launch.

Quartz is very Zen – a synthesis of 'deep thought and a series of cool moves',[3] 'the kind of media most business writers would love to be part of'.[4] It is much admired in the industry for the Koan-esque complicated simplicity that pervades its operations from hiring policy to technology choices, and the intrinsic coherence between these elements. It was launched by Atlantic Media as an independent start-up in September 2012, and its headquarters are in New York, with offices in San Francisco and London. Quartz India was launched in June 2014 in partnership with GE and with a journalistic staff managed by a third-party partner, Scroll.in.

Quartz had 10.9 million monthly unique visitors for October 2014 and its comScore monthly uniques for October were 8.3 million.[5] Owned by the Atlantic Media Group, it has yet to make a profit, but revenues for the first half of 2014 were up 400% on the year before.[6] In October 2014, Quartz staff broke down as follows:[7] 40 journalists; 13 designers, developers, data journalists; and 40 staff on the digital commercial team.

Disrupt thyself

> We imagined ourselves as a venture-capital-backed start-up in Silicon Valley whose mission was to attack and disrupt The Atlantic [...] In essence, we brainstormed the question, 'What would we do if the goal was to aggressively cannibalise ourselves?'[8]

In 2009, the Atlantic Media Company, under the then president Justin Smith, held a meeting to define their future strategy.[9] The *Atlantic Monthly* is a 'storied' (the preferred US media term for legacy, it seems) intellectual magazine that campaigned for abolition and has the distinction of being the first publisher of 'The Battle Hymn of the Republic' in 1862. Around 150 years later the group, recognising it needed to reinvent itself for the digital age, did this by 'pretending it was a Silicon Valley start-up that needed to kill itself to survive'.[10] Three overarching strategic priorities emerged from the meeting: (1) they wanted to be a growth company, rather than one passively managing the shift from print to digital; (2) digital should lead everything; and (3) they should focus on decision-makers and influential people.

These goals led to the creation of a portfolio of media online sites ranging from a digital version of *The Atlantic*, to Atlantic Media Strategies, an independent division offering digital advertising and marketing services ranging from analytics to social media campaigns and native advertising.[11]

Quartz was another result: a diversification from the core Atlantic stable that was designed from the outset as a digital-only, mobile-first business news site that offers serious reporting and analysis, aimed at educated, senior-level, international individuals who travel a lot and are interested in global business issues. Members of this group are heavy consumers of digital content, access the internet on many devices, many of them mobile, and are heavy readers of magazines.

Quartz content would be free, supported by a limited amount of high-quality advertising and sponsorship. It would be run as a start-up, and thus bypass the painful process of transforming an existing legacy organisation and the burdens of legacy infrastructure or legacy costs. It would innovate in step with digital media technology and consumption and be able to scale its organisation in step with growth in income and audience.

> One of the critical components of a strong media business is being absolutely right-sized on the cost side [...] What you see a lot of the struggling legacy players dealing with now is trying to retro-fit their cost structures to a completely new paradigm.[12]

A year after its launch it won a Digital General Excellence award from the Society of American Business Editors and Writers. Their commendation neatly summarises the Quartz approach:

> Quartz set itself apart with its deft combination of modern methods and traditional storytelling, and with its commitment to both real-time analysis and longer-form enterprise reporting.[13]

Capture the smart, young, and bored at work

Quartz thus had a clear concept, strategy, and target market from the start. This provided:

> A reason for being, that helps you focus on who your audience is and how you serve them, is an often unstated part. Having a purpose or a mission, rather than just aggregating the eyeballs. That's a big piece of it.[14]

According to Lauf, Quartz's content concept is underpinned by two assumptions.[15] These direct how it writes its stories, the look and feel of the site, how visual elements are used, and how all of these come together on digital devices.

- First, a quality digital news site needs to succeed primarily with the SYBAWs – the 'smart, young, and bored at work'. Sites that fail to resonate strongly with this group 'are dead'. Key content areas for this group are business, technology, finance, and design.

- Second, news consumption has moved from pull (where readers actively go and get news by buying a bundle of stories in a newspaper or visiting a newspaper homepage that offers a set menu of content) to push (where news stories find their way to their audience via social media and mobile notifications). SYBAWs increasingly assume that any news important to them will also find them. Quartz content therefore needs an extremely strong presence in the social streams that SYBAWs use to consume news, and their stories need to be able to stand and travel alone.

Performance data suggest they are meeting these targets. Half its readers come from the US, and the balance from the UK, Canada, Australia, India, and Germany. Their median age is 40, and 40% have an average household income of over $100,000, higher than *The Economist*, the *Wall Street Journal*, *Financial Times*, and *Forbes*.[16] The majority of readers are male (over 70%), with a bias towards tech workers; 40% of the traffic is mobile, with smartphone usage dominating tablets 4:1, particularly in the morning; 15% of Quartz's traffic comes via the homepage, search referrals currently deliver around 25% of traffic and the rest and majority of Quartz's traffic comes from social sharing via Twitter, Facebook, Google+, and Pinterest, as well as from 'dark social' (links sent via online chat or email).

Will it travel?

The joint import of these governing assumptions is that (a) Quartz content needs an extremely strong presence in the social streams that SYBAWs use to consume news, and (b) to make this happen Quartz stories need to be able to stand and travel alone.

> We're founded on the idea that most of our stories are going to make their way in the world through social media, and that's a fairly obvious presumption when you are starting from zero [...] if nobody knows your brand name and nobody knows the website, then you don't expect much traffic from there, [you] expect that people will come to you from social, so that had a lot of influence on the way that we designed the website to start with, because we basically did not have a homepage. (Interviewee)

BuzzFeed's mantra is 'will it share?'. Quartz's is very similar – 'will it travel?' – and Quartz content is designed to be inherently social. Short works on social. Nuggets suit social. Nuggets make headlines that share well. Journalists are encouraged to focus on the headline from early on, thinking always how they will work on social media. According to Lauf, finding 'the atomic' that will grab attention 'doesn't mean that the story can't widen, but think of the headline first ... Will it travel?'[17]

So Quartz content is written to ensure it works on social media. This means many stories are short (see below), and that writers focus on finding 'nuggets', or 'atomics' (see below also), the arresting facts that prompt sharing and also make ideal headlines.

> So much of our traffic opportunity is social, so that pushes you to write
> for humans [...] We want to write headlines people click on. That compels
> you to write good content.[18]

Snappy/short or long/analytical, but always a well-defined angle

> We want to be short, fast and creative. And we want to do longer,
> ambitious stories [that have] higher impact [...] We don't want to do stuff
> in between.[19]

Stories tend to be short (300–600 words), the result of Delaney's V curve analysis (which itself went viral within the world of digital media watchers). This shows how virality in social media is driven by a combination of length, depth, and timeliness.[20] In terms of length, Delaney concluded stories need either to be brief and focused – under 500 words – or long-form – over 1,000 words. Reporters can do both, but should be intentional about it. And short does not mean simple:

> Conversational, global, digital, and smart. Treat readers' time well. Above
> all, don't talk down to the readers. And don't take yourself too seriously.[21]

Quartz has achieved a distinctive editorial voice, often with a surprising 'non-business angle'[22] (see 'What the Top US Engineering Schools have in Common with Hogwarts'[23]), again part of the Delaney philosophy. 'What we aim for is a voice that's smart but doesn't take itself too seriously.'[24]

Short articles predominate, because they work for the limited attention spans of Quartz's busy SYBAWs, and of digital readers in general who tend not to read to the end of long articles. The imperative is to avoid the 'death zone' between 500 and 800 words – too long to be shared, but not long enough to provide real benefit to readers.

'Stop clearing your throat'

The other part of the pared down part is what we emphasise to our writers, which is say what's necessary and no more. I in particular am a very aggressive kind of editor and we spend a lot of time teaching people to not clear their throats at the beginning of an article but just get to the point. 'Say what you need to say and get out of it.' 'If you can use a chart instead of some words, use a chart. Whatever makes it more useful and easier to absorb and basically more efficient for the reader.' So one of our number one tenets is respect the reader's time. Do not do something that wastes their time, and that influences a lot, because on the internet attention, people's time, is the scarce resource. (Interviewee)

Stories can be short if journalists learn to write directly and 'get to the meat'. An element of the Quartz philosophy is that restricting the length and including strong visual elements boost content quality. It forces journalists to 'think through what's most important in the stories, not just process the news',[25] and find a well-defined angle. They are encouraged to 'dive deep', searching for an unlikely piece of data in a story that gets to the heart of a subject[26] and can carry a headline arresting enough to prompt sharing:

There's that one nugget in every story, whether it's a data point, an angle on the story or philosophy, that hasn't been done to death and happens to make things really travel on the social web [...] when you orient your story around a nugget like that this is the kind of stuff that can really travel around the social web.[27]

An archetypical example is '59 Percent of America's Tuna Isn't Actually Tuna',[28] the heading of a 2013 article that reported on mislabelling of fish for sale in the US, which drew on scientific genetic test data from a non-profit ocean protection group called Oceana.

Be visual

We try to tell stories with images and pictures and avoid two extra paragraphs or 70 extra words where a chart or graphic would do. Over 50% of Quartz content has a chart or graph.[29]

This is another mantra. Visual means a minimalist design: pared down with a clean aesthetic, an extremely simple layout that is designed to be intuitive to use and has very few navigation devices. Visual also means an emphasis on strong visual elements, using charts where possible (see below) and large, strong images. White space is used to give stories room to breathe.

Stories load automatically in a continuous 'river'. Originally there was no homepage, and there still is not a homepage equivalent to most digital news organisations (see below). Instead, one story flows into the next, as with social media feeds, with the most important story appearing first.

This is an upmarket home for advertising, and indeed advertising is intended to add to the quality of the user experience. A 'Piccadilly Circus of drop downs, pushovers and distractions' is not for Delaney: 'The ads must be high quality. They are in our news stream, not on the side. They are big and functional.'[30] The centrality of design and the importance of aesthetics became evident in the publications Quartz interviewees saw as making up their competitive set. The standard business publications were mentioned – *The Economist* (of course), the *Financial Times*, the *Wall Street Journal*, and *Forbes* – but also a group of magazines where the visual is intrinsic to the content: *Wallpaper*, *Vogue*, *Vanity Fair*, and *Matter*.

'Charts are our version of cat videos'[31]

Charts are integral to the Quartz content formula: they are visual, share well, and cut to the chase, making the message easier to absorb for busy readers. Journalists are required to use charts where they can and to help them Quartz has developed a tool, Chartbuilder, that allows them to create their own charts (buttressing its commitment to charts, Quartz has even launched an annual 'Chart of the Year' competition).

Journalists are encouraged to research data for charts as much as for stories. Delaney tells PR agencies to 'Pitch me data, don't pitch me a story' – reflecting the belief that Quartz has the better skills to find the story in the data. For an example see 'Which US States Tip the Most (and Least)' (subtitle, 'Delaware: The Stingy State'), the result of Quartz analysis of state data on tipping behaviour.[32]

'Not much of a homepage'

Another component of the core concept is that the content needs to look good on all platforms, especially mobile devices, and it needs to be accessible without apps. The site was designed first for tablets, then for mobile, and finally for desktops.

> *Our cardinal design principles have always been to stay out of your way, let the stories shine, and make sure it all works well on your phone.*[33]

Initially Quartz had no homepage. Readers who did not enter the site through the 'side door' (via email or social media), but via the traditional 'front door', the desktop website, dropped straight into the top story in the Quartz river of articles. This reflected Quartz's conviction about the ascendancy of push over pull (see above): if news websites are not read in a linear way, and readers find articles via referrers in social media or a daily newsletter, then homepages are becoming ever less important.

> *There are people who are extremely loyal to Quartz [... and] don't come to us via the homepage. They follow us on Twitter or on Facebook [...] others see lots of links to Quartz shared in their feed because their friends read us and they end up coming to us several times a day and feel like they are very loyal to us even if they never type qz.com into their address box.*[34]

'The Daily Brief' and then 'a bit of a website' after all

'A bit of a website' (interviewee) was introduced with a site redesign in 2014. This new front door is not a classic homepage in the sense of a start destination for readers, but rather a web version of its morning email the 'The Daily Brief'. This offers a quick summary of key stories in 'Your World Right Now', and should function as 'a well written memo from a trusted advisor'[35] that is intended to be read straight through and sits above the river of stories.

The Daily Brief is sent to over 70,000 subscribers in three editions (US, Europe, and Asia) early in the morning and has a 40–50% open rate.[36] Typically pared back in approach, it is 800 words in length, has no images and comprises a highly selective combination of links to Quartz's own content and curated articles from elsewhere that covers key events that occurred 'while you were sleeping'.

With its newsletter Quartz is trying to become a daily habit for busy readers. The balance of curated to home-grown articles can be surprising. On 23 June 2014 the newsletter had 23 links in total, of which only five came from Quartz. This is not viewed as problematic. In the words of an interviewee: 'audiences aren't stupid. They know there's a big wide web out there'.

Obsessions – 'where important meets interesting'

> One of our guiding principles is our 'obsessions' – the topics we follow closely that mark big shifts in the global economy. This year we've been obsessed, among other things, with Alibaba's IPO, Hong Kong's revolution, ebola, the next billion internet users, Modinomics, and the future of TV-watching. We launched Quartz India – a stand-alone site that is an obsession in itself.[37]

Quartz's 'obsessions' are at times an idiosyncratic variant of newsbeats. They provide the site taxonomy and are now part of the Quartz signature.[38] Delaney got the idea from publications like *New York Magazine*[39] and since introduced by Quartz the concept is growing in popularity. In summer 2014 the *Atlanta Journal-Constitution* restructured its newsroom in an obsession structure,[40] acknowledging it was adapting Quartz's approach. 'Obsessions' are featured as a discrete link on the opening screen. Some obsessions remain relatively constant ('energy shocks', 'the sea', 'glass', 'the next billion'), others emerge in response to topical events and can later disappear (Ukraine, ebola, the Eurocrunch):

> Obsessions. The idea around that has evolved somewhat over time. The original idea was they we would find topics that were really important and represented a phase shift or some moving global phenomenon and we would try to make those our beats and report them obsessively and really report them out. It turned out to be very hard to find out topics that are

simultaneously interesting enough to lots of people and generate enough news to be worth reporting on continuously. And that we care about enough. So in the end obsessions have ended up being not beats as much as markers for areas that we're interested in, and we don't focus exclusively on those. An obsession could be the Hong Kong protest and we would really focus on the reporting. It would be fairly limited in time. There are some areas that only one or two people are interested in. One of our reporters happens to be obsessed with over-fishing and marine life and she's been doing an awful lot on that. It's done well for us and she's tied it into climate change, and into commerce and trade and so it feels like a Quartzy topic if you like. And so she writes that and it's great, and no one else really touches the subject. And then there are others where lots of people chime in. It doesn't matter. It's not very territorial. (Interviewee)

Obsessions bring benefits. They add distinctiveness to the site and provide freedom for journalists. They can pursue personal obsessions as long as they can be tied, however loosely, to international economics.[41] This boosts motivation and in turn content quality and allows Quartz to make best use of its editorial expertise. It can cover a wide news territory with a small staff. According to Delaney:

The vision I had was of a guard standing watching an empty fort [...] if you are covering European bonds and nothing happens for six months there's nothing to write about. We can redeploy that resource.[42]

Staff

We're looking for an ability to write well, curiosity and enthusiasm. They just need to be curious and interested in some subjects. We almost don't mind so much which ones. We hire some people for expertise [...] If we were going to hire someone for religion, say, what would interest us is their level of their curiosity and passion about stuff. It's, you know, having a feeling for the internet and the way that it works. We place quite a lot of importance on the personality and being able to work well in this team of people and as part of this office [...] I suppose that it's easier to say what we're not looking for. Which is people who are very pedigreed but have very, very rigid ways of working, are the ones that have done the least well here [...] people who are very experienced in traditional news organisations [...] are just too rigid and too wedded to 'this is how you do a story and this what a story is and this is how you report it, and this is what a beat is and these are what my areas of interest are'. They just don't function. People have to be willing to go out of their area of interest and cross beat boundaries, and as I said, just be curious. (Interviewee)

The Quartz 'smart but conversational' tone requires experienced staff. Many are pedigreed journalists from established publications including the *Wall Street Journal, Forbes, Business Insider, Wired, The Economist,* and *Time.* Kevin Delaney prefers his journalists to speak at least two languages fluently – the launch team had experience of working in 119 countries and spoke in total 19 different languages. In July 2014 Quartz announced plans to add 30 more journalists, as part of its strategy to increase the volume of stories on the site.[43]

Editorial staff and developers sit together,[44] and 'a lot of the editorial team can code' (interviewee). Journalists produce complete story packages including links, headlines, and photos that have been cropped and adjusted for publication, all of which are ready to be processed by editors. The 'Things Team' of multidisciplinary and multiplatform journalists do the work of a graphics desk. The editorial team watch what is being shared on social channels and capture what is trending for the Top News section (note, this is done by people, not algorithms).

'Technology shapes the way we do journalism'

As a clean sheet and young organisation, Quartz has benefited from being able to set up its technical infrastructure from scratch. A central tenet is that Quartz must work – and look good – on any device: desktop, tablet, and smartphone. This mandates a responsive design, which means the site automatically configures itself depending on the kind of device and screen size a reader is using.

It does not have apps (saving itself the cost of building, managing, and maintaining native apps on multiple platforms); rather it runs on the web browsers mobile devices already have. To achieve this it has developed an independent platform. This brings the benefit of complete control over how it is accessed and means Quartz does not need to work with app stores.

Its content management system (CMS) is WordPress, a widely used open-source blogging tool and CMS that is known for its simplicity; it is easy to learn, easy to use, versatile, and many journalists already know how to use it. Those that do not can pick it up quickly, and new features can be introduced faster than with a customised CMS.

The programming language is HTML5. This provides a common interface that makes loading elements easier and is designed to support multimedia on mobile devices. This works well for news, but it does mean Quartz cannot use CPU-intensive elements like complex graphics or games.

Quartz developed its own tool, Chartbuilder, which allows all journalists, even those not particularly gifted in tech or design, to create charts of publishable quality. Journalists simply put the data series into the tool and select the kind of chart they want. Chartbuilder was opensourced in 2013 along with the underlying charting library, Gneisschart,[45] and has been taken up by the *Wall Street Journal*, the *New Yorker*, FiveThirtyEight, NPR, and others. In 2014 it won first prize for the best publishing technology at the Digiday Awards.

'Advertising should add to the quality of the user experience'[46]

> If the audience is high-demo, its ad sell comes down to a single word that Atlantic Media brandishes well: influentials [...] its pitch is not based simply on wealth or spending ability, but that its readers as [sic] deciders, agenda setters, and idea connectors [...] Quartz is a high end play, differentiating itself from the more mass-orientated Business Insider and Forbes.com.[47]

The Quartz business model is free access supported by advertising (here its formula departs from *The Economist*'s, which has a metred paywall); it combines display ads and native advertising, although Lauf has indicated he would like to develop some kind of paid option at some future point.[48]

> It was a difficult decision to have fewer ads per page, but the ads we have are higher value. (Interviewee)

Placing ads in the news stream, with plenty of white space, means they can be large and stand out but at the same time, assuming the quality criteria are met, they should not intrude. This gives 'partners an even better canvas on which to tell their stories'.[49]

It seems like an easy throwaway, but quality of content matters. Quality of design interface matters. Quality of ads matters [...] We feel vindicated; it's a hallmark of what we do, and it's proven to be useful. Users actually like ads if they're good. Sounds very Jonah Peretti, but it is true.[50]

Quartz has an upmarket readership and its 'river of stories' format means there are relatively few slots for advertising, meaning by extension that Quartz's ad revenue stream is capped. Scarcity coupled with an upmarket demographic and high interaction rates mean Quartz can charge high ad rates.

Atlantic Media Company helped initially attract premium advertisers (Chevron, Boeing, Credit Suisse, and Cadillac). Quartz now has around 45 regular advertisers, of which 40% are in financial services, and renewal rates are 80%. CPM rates are reputedly between two and four times higher for native than for banner ads.[51] Developing metrics to demonstrate impact of advertising has been a priority for Quartz – for example, they use interaction rates as an alternative to the standard clickthrough rates.

We have to convince advertisers that actually the readers who spend time on this page are worth more and should be measured differently from what they are used to measuring, and that means a very tight understanding between the editorial side and the commercial side about why we do this and what the value of it is and can advertisers be convinced of that, and can the site reach enough scale to make it worthwhile to have that conversation with advertisers. All of these become very, very tied together and that's where these blends come in. That's why these things have to work together. (Interviewee)

Branded content is designed to blend into the mainstream journalistic content in terms of quality, style, tone, and presentation, but is clearly labelled as such. As with the *New York Times*, enormous effort is put into native content which should be equivalent in quality to journalistic content (a typical example is, '25 Ways We Saw the World Change in 2013' from Goldman Sachs). Quartz has a stand-alone team of copywriters and designers working on branded content. The team work together with advertisers, with the extent of collaboration ranging from developing the ideas to execution or tech integration. Data from Quartz suggest it has an equivalent number of staff in this area as journalists.

I started out as a journalist, a wide-eyed idealist, and I'm still a wide-eyed idealist. I still believe deeply what we're doing on the business side is essential and important work. Intellectually, honest journalism is the underpinning for a democratic society. If we can figure out how to make this commercially valuable for hundreds of years, we all win.[52]

Conferences aimed at exclusive audiences are a newer revenue stream. The advertising and sponsorship income they generate amounts to around 10% of total revenues.[53] The first 'Quartz Live' conference, 'The Next Billion', was held in Seattle in 2014 (and sold out) and underwritten by Intel; six further events are planned for 2015.

The netsuke of digital news

The Quartz concept is very simple and its model is entirely coherent: target market, commercial concept, tone of voice, visual style, hiring strategy, and technology choices all dovetail perfectly. Quartz is very innovative, but the innovation is subtle. It lies in its selectivity, in the reflection, the tweaking, and the refining of those elements it has chosen to combine. It lies also in how it has woven these core elements together to create a whole that delivers much more than the component parts.

Quartz is distinctive and successful, but has profited from the fact that 'quality competitors left some daylight'; that is, they were slow to move into business news for the mobile social era. That fact has now been comprehensively noted, and Quartz will face more competition for its sophisticated high-income readers.

Quartz is a niche player and this may prove to be its dilemma. It is out of the start-up mode and needs to scale up. It must post more content – and slots for advertising – in order to acquire more readers and advertisers. But in doing so it could well hit the boundaries of its 'high end' niche, and dilute the purity of its organisational/editorial formula. If it does not want to dilute the formula it will need to add additional revenue streams (thus the event business) and/or it may need to add paid product (thus the comments by Lauf). Either way, it faces a Koan-esque challenge of needing to grow yet not dilute the sophisticated focus that makes it unique.

5

BuzzFeed – Making Life More Interesting for the Hundreds of Millions Bored at Work

There's not a lot of people making content for the way people consume it today [...] you have these massive tech companies and these massive platforms [...] and then you have giant media companies that are focused on industrial era forms of production [...] and people increasingly on a Tuesday night are saying 'I want to spend time on my Facebook news feed', 'I want to spend time on YouTube' [...] on media being created by this much larger world of producers where social is helping you find stuff that you are going to really like, and machine learning is helping recommend things to you, and that stream is as engaging and exciting as watching a piece of highly expensively produced media behind a paywall [...] but there are very few media companies making media for that stream and [...] that's where you see this huge disconnect between the tech industry and the news industry because the media industry can't actually provide the stuff that the tech industry needs.[1]

BuzzFeed is a young social media native. 'The Web's king of viral content',[2] Jonah Peretti, founded it in 2006 as a side project to his role at the Huffington Post which he had co-founded a year earlier. Peretti was a parallel entrepreneur until 2011 when AOL bought the Huffington Post and he switched to focus on BuzzFeed alone.

BuzzFeed is privately owned and solidly financed, having received $96.3 million in five rounds of funding from 13 investors.[3] The last and largest round was $50 million in 2014 from Andreessen Horowitz, representing a putative company valuation of $850 million. Reportedly Disney tried to buy BuzzFeed in 2014, but was put off by an asking price of over $1 billion.

BuzzFeed has the highest number of global monthly uniques of all the organisations profiled here, reportedly over 200 million.[4] BuzzFeed became profitable in 2013. Advertising revenues for 2014 were reputedly over $100 million.[5] Headquartered in New York, BuzzFeed employs 750 staff, with offices in Los Angeles, Washington, DC, San Francisco, Chicago, London, Berlin, Sydney, and Mumbai, and teams in São Paulo and Paris. There are around 250 reporters and writers across BuzzFeed News, Life and Buzz, with around 120 working just in news. Data scientists number around 100, and there are 'a lot' in tech. BuzzFeed Video has over 60 producers based in LA.[6]

Peretti's viral content lab in Chinatown

Peretti is described as a 'quintessential nerd genius', and his initial vision for BuzzFeed was an experimental 'viral-content skunkworks'[7] that would track viral memes and identify, using data analysis techniques, which characteristics made users want to send a piece of content on to others.[8]

Peretti is neither ex-businessperson nor ex-journalist. A graduate of the MIT Media Lab, he has taught on NYI's Interactive Telecommunications programme and for the Parsons School of Design. Before the Huffington Post he was Director of R&D at Eyebeam, a non-profit art and technology centre that develops tools for digital research and experimentation. Long fascinated by 'contagious media', he first came to the public eye through a series of contagious media experiments, of which the best known is probably the Nike ID Sweatshop Email.

In 2001 Peretti ordered a pair of customised Nike sneakers, embroidered with the word 'sweatshop'. Nike cancelled the order, triggering a series of emails between Peretti and Nike. Peretti forwarded these to friends, who in turn passed them on and eventually the email exchange reached the attention of traditional media, and Peretti was interviewed on *NBC Today* along with a Nike spokesperson. A month later Peretti (then still at MIT) published an online essay about the experience ('Culture, Jamming, Memes, Social Networks, and the Emerging Media Ecology'), and a statistical analysis of the email traffic.[9] This anecdote (or meme?) underlines how atypical BuzzFeed's roots are for a news organisation: they extend down into academia, science (epidemiology and data analysis), and into technology (the MIT Media Lab and Silicon Valley).

Peretti ticks all the boxes for a classic charismatic leader and his conceptual approach is stamped on all aspects of his organisation. He is a visionary who saw an opportunity in an emergent field and built an organisation capable of grasping it. He is a natural communicator who has constructed a compelling narrative to explain the BuzzFeed concept. He appears to be an intuitive strategist who has helped create two of the world's leading digital media organisations, who seems able to distil the salient learnings out of history, theory, and personal experience and turn these into a business plan.

'We built a locomotive and a few days later the train tracks got built'

The first stage in the BuzzFeed life cycle was BuzzBot, an instant messaging client that analysed feeds from blogs to detect which were accelerating fastest and sent users a link to them. Next came a website for 'contagious media' featuring some of the most popular links. The logical next step was to move on to create original content explicitly designed for sharing.

> A big part of our recent success has also been luck. People don't like to admit it but skill is 63% luck [...] It's like we happened to start surfing a few minutes before a great wave rolled in. Or we built a locomotive and a few days later the train tracks got built. We were obsessed with social content and ads before anyone else cared and it was extremely lucky that the world shifted toward us when it did.[10]

BuzzFeed's timing was excellent – it was perfectly placed to exploit the convergence between social and mobile (social users tend to be mobile users) and the spread of mobile devices and consumption. When Peretti founded BuzzFeed, Twitter did not exist and Facebook was in its infancy. By the time he left the Huffington Post to concentrate on BuzzFeed full-time, Twitter and Facebook had reached critical mass and the social/mobile era had arrived. BuzzFeed could rise naturally with the social media tide.

In 2015 it plans to launch dedicated apps for news and video as well as new products, such as BFF, which will create content specifically for social media platforms.

'BuzzFeed is the best at melding tech and journalism'

> The biggest difference is that you get a tremendous amount of data back about what consumers are reading and what they are sharing [...]

> *sharing has always been the biggest metric because it shows that someone thinks that a piece of content is worth passing on to a friend. You've always had [...] word of mouth where people watching a television show they really like go and tell their friends [...] but [...] distribution was tied to these massive industrial era models and then you have a little word of mouth as extra. And now it's been kind of inverted [...] word of mouth is the distribution [...] you are getting so much data back about what people like and what people share and that can immediately inform the media you create.*[11]

The lightweight nature of much BuzzFeed content belies the sophistication of the processes used to create it. At heart, BuzzFeed is about data science, about analysing user data to decode how and why content is shared and distributed. User data are captured, analysed, and manipulated in a perpetual loop of analysis, interpretation, experimentation, feedback, and refinement. BuzzFeed's goal is to identify which characteristics have a predictive relationship with virality, maximise these and thus accelerate the 'spread rate' of its content. They clearly have gone some way towards decoding virality – in March 2014 the total number of interactions (likes, comments, and shares) on Facebook for BuzzFeed articles was over 47 million (the Huffington Post came second with 29 million; Dailymail.co.uk had 8 million).[12]

'Will it share?'

Natural language processing techniques are used to understand what elements perform best. Different versions of headlines are uploaded to see which generate the best click rates and alternative images are uploaded to see which are shared the most. Key learnings are applied across categories – insights from lists are applied to quizzes, successful quiz concepts are applied to social advertising campaigns.

The centrality of data science is captured perfectly by the recent choice of publisher. The role has gone to Dao Nguyen, the data scientist previously responsible for using data analysis to drive BuzzFeed's expansion.

> *Dao is a new type of publisher. She isn't the heir to a newspaper baron and she won't be responsible for the business, selling ads, or physical newsstand distribution. Instead, she'll lead publishing for the social web, in the most modern sense, where data science, the CMS, technology, and*

a deep understanding of social networks, mobile devices, and digital video matter most. If publishing is 'the activity of making information available to the general public', then I'm confident Dao will become the very best publisher in a rapidly changing industry where technology and data science are the key to success.[13]

While data reign supreme, they do not decide everything. Peretti shares Jeff Bezos's preference for investing in the long term (the parallels are particularly striking in the IT area). BuzzFeed should 'avoid anything that is bad for our readers and can only be justified by short term business interests'.[14]

We could juice our traffic and revenue by dropping everything and focusing entirely on the short term. And that is what companies do when they are trying to flip for a fast payday. But when you are building something enduring, you have to care as much about next year as you do about next week. That is how you build something big and that's our goal.[15]

Peretti is committed to growth and even sees BuzzFeed taking on aspects of legacy media's mantle. But his growth corridor is clearly defined: he is discriminating about which aspects of legacy media's terrain interest him:

Now that we are a much bigger operation the challenge is staying focused despite the distractions being offered by traditional media companies. My big goal for 2014 is not to do a BuzzFeed TV show.[16]

We will NOT launch a white labeled version of BuzzFeed to power other sites or a BuzzFeed social network – we'll leave that to pure tech companies in Silicon Valley. We will NOT launch a print edition or a paywall or a paid conference business – we'll leave that to other publications. We have a great business model that has a bright future as social and mobile continue to become the dominate form of media consumption. We will stay away from anything that requires adopting a legacy business model, even a lucrative one like cable syndication fees or prime time television ads [...] We need to stay patient and focused.[17]

(Since making this statement, BuzzFeed has launched BuzzFeed Motion Pictures, but despite the name this is a far cry from a Hollywood studio.

It has also made a foray into live events with its BuzzFeed Brew interview series.)

BuzzFeed's formula – for the organisation as much as for the content – synthesises insights from different fields – the historical development of the media industry and its business models, Silicon Valley and tech industry organisations, data science and the causes of virality. The challenge for legacy players trying to compete is the breadth of expertise this formula draws on:

> It's funny when you hear people say, 'It's a terrible thing for the news industry [...] we need these monopolies that are impossible to compete with and that's what's good for society'. It actually is much more complicated than that and when you look at the way that technology can provide competitive advantage for companies today, different but bigger barriers to entry, having a site that runs quickly, having an advertising model that works on mobile, having a good data science team that can give you better insights [...] certain network properties, once you have a certain level of scale there are things like preferential attachment and network theory that suggest that it becomes easier to reach an audience. All those things come together and I don't think that people understand very well, but it does make it possible to build a defensible business and that's why we've been able to grow so quickly, generate profits, while simultaneously investing in correspondents and an investigative news team and other things that people thought it wasn't possible for internet companies to invest in.[18]

Innovation à la Silicon Valley

In some respects, BuzzFeed is a tech company with a media layer on top. Peretti's default reference group tends to be the tech sector:

> Some of the stuff that Google has done and Apple has done has been very inspirational to us, in terms of how we run the company and some of the way we organise the company [...] and some of the things that you associate more with start-up companies, have had a great effect on what we're able to do, even though we're, in many ways, a media company.[19]

BuzzFeed applies many standard tech industry practices: release fast, learn, iterate, canary development (where new ideas are released alongside existing versions to allow new features to be trialled without changing the main user experience).

Interdisciplinary small teams are the basic organisational building block:

> We have been able to grow quickly without major organisational breakdowns by attracting great people and trusting them to do great work. The best work comes from small groups of smart people with considerable autonomy and the ability to collaborate freely with others when it makes sense.[20]

The core organisational departments are culture, news, technology, product, and data (including a non-relational realtime statistic collection, a machine learning system for predicting viral hits, and publishing tools for editors). Collaboration between product, tech, and editorial areas is a priority:

> We will continue our R&D focused on inventing and advancing media formats. This requires ongoing interdisciplinary effort combining product, tech, and editorial.[21]

BuzzFeed plans to expand further internationally. It follows a tech industry model and will:

> internationalise like a tech company, not a media company. We won't launch different sites in different markets, or the equivalent of "local newspapers" in every market. We will have one big global site that will dynamically change to meet the needs of different countries and languages [...] Web culture is global, youth culture is global, news is global, and this provides a clear path for BuzzFeed to globalise as well.[22]

Pillars of BuzzFeed content

BuzzFeed's core content areas are:[23]

- BuzzFeed Editorial, which has three divisions: (1) Buzz, home of the listicles, quizzes, and cats, (2) News, which is expanding rapidly, and (3) Life, which has lifestyle content – DIY, food and style. All report to Ben Smith.
- BuzzFeed Motion Pictures.

- BuzzFeed Distributed, which creates bite-sized content solely for emerging platforms such as Tumblr, Instagram, Snapchat, Vine, and messaging apps, and was established in response to the teen shift away from Facebook.
- BuzzFeed Creative, which is responsible for branded content for advertisers. It has 60 creatives and 15 branded video producers.

While even serious subjects can be turned into genuinely amusing content (see '10 Cardboard Boxes that Look Like David Cameron' or '8 Basic Steps to Rejecting a Takeover Offer'), underlying the frivolity are deep reflections on the psychology of sharing. Peretti believes sharing viral content serves a fundamental and universal human need to connect, and can bring three types of benefit: an emotional 'gift' or reaction for the recipient (a new idea, stress relief, happiness, or sadness), the transmission of information (facts about things the recipient likes, proving an argument, etc.), and a boost to the sharer's identity or community membership.

BuzzFeed's combination of scientific thoroughness and millennial froth is encapsulated in its internal style guide, which was published to plaudits from *Time* and the *Guardian* in 2014. This gives insights into the concerns of BuzzFeed's audience (-ass and -shaming should be hyphenated, while -bait, -butt, and -fest should not) as well as into how seriously their interests are taken (see the detailed section on LGBT terminology).

Respect for the user experience is built into many general content principles. Scrollable lists are preferred to slideshows, which irritate because they require repeated clicks (and they also function poorly on mobile). BuzzFeed eschews clickbait (misleading or manipulative headlines) since these are counterproductive – 'you can trick someone to click, but you cannot trick someone to share'. Indeed their headline strategy goes in the opposite direction – 'make fairly small promises and then overdeliver'.[24]

'It's actually harder to make the definitive cat list than to do most journalism'[25]

If Peretti is King of Viral Content, then BuzzFeed is King of Listicles, which are the mainstay of its Buzz content category. The most visited content for 2013 was '30 Signs You're Almost 30'. Peretti notes that lists have an august heritage encompassing the Ten Commandments and the Bill of Rights. Editor-in-chief Ben Smith explains that lists are cognitively intrinsically satisfying because they organise information in a way that mirrors how our brains process data. More prosaically, lists also work well on mobile, helping share rates to rise even higher.

Interactive quizzes also feature prominently. According to a press release 7.2 billion quiz questions were answered in 2014.[26] 'What State Do You Actually Belong In?' was one the biggest posts ever with over 42 million views. These generate high levels of involvement (users like to find out about themselves, and many users take them more than once) and sharing (users like to tell others more about themselves). They also work well on mobile.

A knee-jerk criticism is the predilection for cats (see 'Twenty-Three Kitties of Congress'). The Poynter Institute actually audited BuzzFeed's cat content in 2014 and found 22,500 pieces 'about or including cats' since it was founded in 2006.[27] Peretti points out that quality media has 'form' in lightweight content also:

> The argument goes along the lines of 'How can I take you seriously if you have a slidey-thing on your site or if you have a list or quiz?' And yet when you look across all traditional media it's always been a mix of serious things and crosswords and cartoons.[28]

Its 'no hater' hiring policy has also provoked criticism. Peretti explains this as follows:

> Being a hater means writing a long thing about how a mediocre movie sucks. And in such a way that makes the author look cool. We don't like that kind of stuff. There was a period on the internet in the mid-2000s when a lots of bloggers were very sarcastic and found everything shit. It was almost a lazy way of criticism. There's lots of mediocre things in the world. Just ignore those things. We're probably more generally positive than other publications. We do not think being critical in itself is a virtue. Being critical of a deserving target and exposing something real is a virtue. But we also think people are looking for things to enjoy and to celebrate. We want to show people things that are worth their time.[29]

Designs on news

BuzzFeed is a textbook disrupter, starting at the bottom of the news content world and then moving swiftly upmarket to threaten leading players in their home territories. During its short life BuzzFeed has morphed from viral content skunkworks into one of the world's largest producers of digital content, from the inane listicle to investigative news. Over 7,000 news stories were published in 2014, with bylines from 20 countries.[30]

News was not part of Peretti's original plan but in 2012 he saw the opportunity to provide serious content alongside the entertainment. News is now a core element of the BuzzFeed mission, and he plans on BuzzFeed becoming the 'leading news source for the social, media, mobile world':[31]

> BuzzFeed has a major role to play in the coming years producing great journalism and compelling entertainment. We have the potential to be a defining company, the same role the traditional media companies played decades ago. These companies were once small and scrappy like us. They faced the scepticism of their incumbents, they pioneered new models, embraced new technologies, and succeeded because they served their audience better than what came before. This is a great aspiration for us as well.[32]

Peretti draws parallels between the start of *Time* in the 1920s and BuzzFeed's beginnings 90 years later:

> Both [...] evolved from our respective early days to become much more ambitious. As Time and BuzzFeed emerged from our respective youths, we both expanded into original reporting, commissioned longform features, and built teams of foreign correspondents. In our case, it only took a few years to go from summarising web trends in our little Chinatown office to reporting from Syria and the Ukraine with local security, body armour, helmets, and satellite phones. And both Time and BuzzFeed grew by creating irresistible lists such as Time's '100 Most Influential People' and BuzzFeed's '42 People You Won't Believe Actually Exist.'[33]

Looking forward, BuzzFeed can fill the vacuum created by the decline of print:

> Despite the struggles of the traditional media, there remains an insatiable desire for great reporting, entertaining content, and powerful storytelling.

Facebook, Twitter, and the other Silicon Valley-based social sites are amazing distribution platforms, but user generated content alone isn't enough to fill the hole left by the ongoing decline of print newspapers and magazines. The world needs sustainable, profitable, vibrant content companies staffed by dedicated professionals; especially content for people that grew up on the web, whose entertainment and news interests are largely neglected by television and newspapers.[34]

BuzzFeed's news is focused on a young demographic that is more or less permanently online. Its coverage has expanded progressively, expanding existing verticals, adding new beats, and taking on new staff. Politics was one of the first news areas, and its coverage of the 2012 US presidential campaign established it as a player in current affairs. Now its news content ranges from climate change and technology, to politics and world events (especially Russia, Ukraine, and the Middle East), from terrorism to LGBT issues. Depth of coverage has expanded also:

We started with cute kittens and Internet memes because that's where the social Web was when the company started [...] We've expanded to things like long-form reporting and scoops because those became a big part of what the social web is all about [...] Our political reporting is so good and we've broken so many stories that those folks are sometimes surprised that we have other stuff on the site.[35]

High-profile journalists have been hired to support this expansion. In the US these include Ben Smith from *Politico*, as Editor-in-Chief across all BuzzFeed content (2011), Lisa Tozzi from the *New York Times* as News Director (2013), Miriam Elder, ex-Moscow Bureau Chief for the *Guardian*, to build foreign coverage and a team of correspondents (2013), Pulitzer Prize-winning investigative reporter Mark Schoofs from ProPublica to establish an investigative unit (2013) and Peter Lauria from Reuters as Business Editor (2013).

More recently BuzzFeed has expanded its UK news operation with hires including Robert Colvile from the *Daily Telegraph* as UK News Director (2014) and Emily Ashton from the *Sun* as Political Correspondent (2014). UK editor Luke Lewis plans to establish a beat structure covering themes such as LGBT, economics, housing, as well as launch investigative reporting and regional coverage, and develop new story formats.[36]

Building BuzzFeed into a news organisation

We don't have the trust the traditional news brands have won over the past 100 years, but we are working hard to earn it, and it won't take us 100 years to get there.[37]

BuzzFeed started where the social web was, which was fun, sharable content. [...] We built an audience. We built a business and we built a new model for advertising. And that is what allowed us to hire Ben Smith. That is what allowed Ben Smith to hire all these talented reporters that he's brought on to the point that we were able to have the budget to have people travel with the Romney campaign, have Michael Hastings covering Obama.[38]

Ben Smith wants BuzzFeed News to advance big stories and make an impact with its reporting. He feels that not only is BuzzFeed a credible news organisation, but it is positioned to be a better news organisation than many because it has the skills to find important stories in the torrent of social media content (see 'Does this Soldier's Instagram Account Prove Russia is Covertly Operating in Ukraine?'), and because it can bring order to the surge of online information that emerges when big news stories break:

There was this illusion pre-Twitter that news wasn't messy [...] But breaking news on any platform [...] has always been messy. And dealing with the chaos – ordering it, prioritising it, deciding what to emphasise and what to underplay – is part of what it means to be a news organisation, particularly in a real-time news environment like the one the web has given us.[39]

The combination of lifestyle content with serious news presents no conflict, nor does it undermine the quality of that news:

We can be very serious about politics and we can be writing about the riots in Ferguson, and we can be very serious about breaking news on that front, we don't have an issue with the fact that people are going to find it immediately above an article from Vice talking about how 'cuddle parties' are not quite what they used to be.[40]

It should be noted that BuzzFeed has run into criticism for the sourcing of its listicles, for plagiarism (the writer was fired), and most recently for retracting 4,000 posts without notification.[41] Peretti attributed these to BuzzFeed's tech origins, and noted that they predate the hiring of Ben Smith. This defence was echoed by Slate's Will Oremus:

> Tech companies do just delete products and pages that are no longer functional or relevant. They view broken or outdated features as 'bad user experience', or bad 'UX'. In the tech world, bad UX is a far greater sin than lacking transparency or usability.[42]

BuzzFeed Motion Pictures

If news was the first big pivot, video was the second. The BuzzFeed YouTube video channel was launched in 2013 and in 2014 had over 200 million monthly views, 1.7 billion YouTube views, and 6.6 million subscribers.[43] BuzzFeed Video expanded into BuzzFeed Motion Pictures in 2014 which is projected to become a mainstay of both content and advertising revenue.[44] BuzzFeed believes 'digital video is the future of the media industry' and intends to shift from short-form video to mid-form serialised video focused on building characters and genres, and is also building a 'Future of Fiction' team to explore the future of long-form television and 'trans-media video'.[45] Much of its last tranche of funding was earmarked for the expansion of its video operation in Los Angeles.

> Video is an area that has just exploded for us [...] I have been frustrated with video for years [...] because we haven't found a way to do the rapid creation of content and then the constant learning from the audience and that's something that you could do with text because it's cheaper to do [...] Video is so expensive that it was difficult to try ideas and experiment [...] Ze Frank [...] has built a tremendous team that has figured out how to make video production much more web-friendly than before, so we have a studio lot in LA, we have built sets for all kinds of scenarios, so a school, an office, a café, a dungeon, whatever you want, and then we have a team that brainstorms ideas for concepts [...] and quickly can shoot videos, release them, and learn from how people respond [...] The fixed costs of our studio are already spent, and the variable cost is almost nothing, so it flips the Hollywood model where the studio lots actually become banks [...] and there's no learning after the project.[46]

Data analysis influences every stage of video production. The content is a mixture of light and serious, all driven by user analysis, experimentation, and testing. Close attention is paid to how and on which platforms material is shared and to comments.[47] Branded video content is also produced for advertisers such as Purina and General Electric.

BuzzFeed Brews

BuzzFeed has also made (as yet low-key) moves into 'people media': 'BuzzFeed Brews', a series of live interviews with key political figures, accompanied by free beer, was launched in 2013 (the beer is intended to get interviewees 'relaxed so they can talk about things people don't normally hear them talk about'[48]). In 2014 the concept was expanded through a collaboration with *CBS This Morning* to include 'newsmakers' in business, entertainment, and pop culture in New York and Los Angeles. The series seeks to deliver a 'full social experience' combining three platforms: live events, on-air, and online. The interviews are livestreamed on BuzzFeed and highlights from the interview featured the following day on *This Morning* and on CBSNews.com.

'Lighting up the social web for advertisers'

BuzzFeed is native advertising only – a response on the part of Peretti to a structural weakness he perceived at the Huffington Post, namely its reliance on SEO, banners, and pre-roll ads, which he felt would never sustain a content business in the long term:

> *Back in my previous company which was the Huffington Post, I didn't know anything about advertising and neither did my partners when we first launched, and we did all this tech development and built a platform [...] and editors had all these tools and all these special things that they could do, and the advertisers [...] would just get banners, so all our tech development did not benefit us as a business at all. At BuzzFeed I wanted to avoid that. I wanted one uniform platform for distributing media and that [...] could be used for news [...] for entertainment [...] for branded content. And then we still created separate teams [...] but they get the benefit of the data science and all the cool formats and all the different*

innovation we are doing on the platform side. The idea was to do what Google did with their product which is to make advertising the inversion of the editorial product where it's powered by the same thing but to have a church–state separation.[49]

Over three-quarters of BuzzFeed's visitors come via recommendations on social networks, over half are aged 18–34, and over half visit on mobile devices. This is an attractive audience for advertisers:

We never really tried to go after that demographic. But those are the people who are most active on social. Those are the people who are sharing. Those are the people who, for whatever reason, flock to our site. They tend to be very educated. They tend to have high incomes. They tend to live in big cities and be the kind of people that are omnivorous about culture and all these different things.[50]

Native content should look and feel like standard BuzzFeed content and be capable of going viral in the same way. It is developed by a separate social advertising division which functions more or less as an ad agency, working directly with brands to develop content in the BuzzFeed style (see 'The 20 Coolest Hybrid Animals' for Toyota, or 'Which David Bowie Are You?' for Spotify). The division comprises a sales team, a creative services team, a social discovery team, and an ad ops team. The standard BuzzFeed CMS is used to distribute and publish content. To smooth the advertiser's path through the native jungle, the BuzzFeed University offers a series of monthly podcasts on YouTube to train brands and agencies in the 'BuzzFeed way'.

Advertisers pay advertising rates around double those commanded by most publishers,[51] and benefit from BuzzFeed's expertise in creating viral content and data analysis and its technology platform:

At BuzzFeed we say 'we'll do a full stack of helping the brand make compelling branded content' [...] they often want to do things that aren't good for the user and aren't in their own self-interest and would be bad for the BuzzFeed site and bad for them as a brand, and we tell them, 'Don't do that! We'll help you do something better.'[52]

While native advertising alarms many, Peretti argues it is a simply a new form of a long-established tradition. He sees a parallel with the competition between the *New York Times* and the *Herald Tribune* at the start of the Second World War:

> *The Times won out because it published garment merchant listings on the front page, winning over advertisers. At the same time, when newsprint was rationed during the war the paper cut ads and kept more stories. It struck the perfect balance between editorial values and business sense. After the war, the Times emerged as the unparalleled paper with more subscribers, more advertising revenue, and became, by many measures, the leading newspaper in the world [...] The obvious lesson from this story is that we need to build a great business while remaining true to our readers and editorial mission.*[53]

He also feels quality advertising content can add value – again, not a new idea for the industry:

> *A magazine like Vogue has really great editorial fashion photography and really great branded fashion photography, and if you ripped all the great ads out the magazine would be a worse magazine [...] the advertising actually adds to the product [...] It just feels like a historic anomaly that you have this fish or fowl thing on the web where banner ads looked and felt and worked totally different to the rest of the content on the site. It just felt bolted on.*[54]

Native-only also positions BuzzFeed excellently for the shift to mobile: banners do not work on mobile devices, while viral ads do:

> *Our ads perform better on mobile! These trends are the reason that BuzzFeed is profitable in the first place. The more content consumption shifts to social and mobile, the better for our business.*[55]

There are indications that BuzzFeed may not stay native-only for ever. Incoming president Greg Coleman intriguingly gave programmatic advertising as a priority:

> *I don't know how we are going to get there. But because BuzzFeed is not accepting any banner ads whatsoever, getting into the world of programmatic is going to take a lot of work, ingenuity and creativity. And maybe we won't get there [...] we are certainly going to put our heads*

together to see if there is a really intelligent way [...] of where we crack that code.[56]

This statement appears to contradict a core element of the BuzzFeed model and Peretti philosophy. But although BuzzFeed is more of a tech company than a media one in many respects, it fails to meet the specification in one critical respect – it lacks the ideal tech-industry scalable business model, where revenues can increase aggressively while costs fall. For BuzzFeed, growth in revenues means growth in costs. Programmatic ad selling could help mitigate this and allow it to continue investing in content creators:

> *Venture capitalists don't like funding companies that have reporters on staff. In the early days of BuzzFeed, I had several VCs say they were interested in investing if we could figure out a way to fire all the editors and still run the site [...] Tech investors prefer pure platform companies because you can just focus on the tech, have the users produce the content for free, and scale the business globally without having to hire many people. Start-ups that promise this vision have an easier time attracting funding which is why there are so many start-ups trying to be the next Twitter or Facebook or Instagram.*[57]

Tech – build the whole enchilada

> *Nobody has built a truly great publishing company for the social age and we have a good shot to be the ones who do it. But it means that we can't take short cuts, we need to always invest in the future, and this is why we spend so much time and money building technology and products that don't have an immediate impact on the company but will help us down the road.*[58]

Notable in this quote are (1) the long-term planning horizon, and (2) the 'build our own' philosophy. BuzzFeed has a full-stack vertical integration tech strategy, meaning it has everything in house and builds its systems itself – it manages its own servers, and has created its own content management system, formats for content and adverts, systems for data capture and analysis and for machine learning. This is a Rolls Royce approach, not open to less well-funded media organisations. The benefits are quality, control, coherence, and not having to rely on external suppliers that may be working with competitors:

71

stapling together products made by other companies [...] This is why so many publisher sites look the same and also why they can be so amazingly complex and hard to navigate. They are Frankenstein products bolted together by a tech team that integrates other people's products instead of building their own.[59]

Again, this policy decision was based on historical analysis:

It is hard to build vertically integrated products because you have to get good at several things instead of just one. This is why for years Microsoft was seen as the smart company for focusing on just one layer and Apple was seen as dumb for trying to do everything. But now Apple is more than twice as valuable as Microsoft and the industry is starting to accept that you need to control every layer to make a really excellent product. Even Microsoft and Google have started to make their own hardware after years of insisting that software is what matters.[60]

'Build your own' leads to strategic advantage and content differentiation:

doing something hard can actually be an advantage for a business. It means that there are not that many other people trying to do what we do or capable of doing what we do.[61]

At base – still investigating why things go viral

BuzzFeed is a tech–media hybrid, and BuzzFeed's content is both an art and a science. The company originated as a lab to test for viral content, and testing still lies at the heart of its activities, driving to understand why things go viral. The organisation has undergone two big pivots. The first was to expand from fluffy entertainment into news. The second was expansion into video. Data science underpins its moves into these areas, and in both cases its commitment is serious.

In addition to its mastery of data science as applied to publishing, BuzzFeed's success lies in a series of subtle, even low-key elements that are extremely well executed and synchronise with each other to fuel growth. It has created a new segment of the media as a result of technological advance and positioned itself to rise with the tide. It has a smart charismatic leader who knows where he wants the organisation to go and is confident enough to share his strategy with the organisation as well as the world at large. It has created a culture where engineers are first-class citizens, alongside journalists. It uses insights from data analysis to create perhaps silly and sponsored content, but uses revenues from these content genres to subsidise serious investigative journalism. It is one of the few media organisations that can make social work for advertisers. It is both well-funded and profitable. And finally, it can (still) move at speed into new areas. These elements in combination make it a challenging competitor.

6

Vice Media – 'We are the Changing of the Guard'[1]

I said to Rupert, 'I have Gen Y, I have social, I have online video. You have none of that. I have the future, you have the past.'[2]

Vice Media is hard to define – even for itself (it describes itself as 'an ever-expanding nebula of immersive investigative journalism, uncomfortable sociological examination, uncouth activities, making fun of people'[3]). It is a twenty-first-century variant of a media conglomerate that produces primarily video content for youth audiences of which an increasingly important element is news. It started off as an alternative street magazine in Montreal, developed relatively swiftly into a leading international producer of online video for Gen Y-ers which it now distributes on online platforms (web and YouTube) but increasingly also via an international array of legacy terrestrial and cable TV channels.

At the heart of Vice is the omnipresent Shane Smith – founder, strategist, sometime foreign correspondent, deal maker, and generator of inspired viral-ready soundbites. Shane Smith's brash contrarian DNA is stamped all over Vice in the same way that Jonah Peretti's is at BuzzFeed. The two leaders' personalities stand at opposing ends of the introvert–extrovert spectrum but share what seems to be an innate entrepreneurial gift for designing organisations and business models that can thrive in a turbulent industry. Shane Smith thinks big:

I've said I want to be the next ESPN, the next CNN and the next MTV rolled up into one [...] everybody says, 'He's a megalomaniac lunatic.' If you look at the numbers you can do on YouTube, if you look, for example at Machinima [an online video network for gamers] with 3.5 billion views a month, you wouldn't be the next CNN. You would be the next CNN 10x. That's what's exciting for us.[4]

He also thinks young:

> *You can't retrofit it. If there's a bunch of old dudes in a boardroom that go, 'OK. Let's start making video', what they try to do is hire pedigreed people. What you get is a shittier version of TV. You really have to rip out the pipes. You have to make things in a different way, hire people who have never worked in TV or commercials or film, get people straight out of schools, get people who don't know what they're doing, form your own school and train these kids. The reason I'm telling you all this, the reason I'm giving away my secrets, is that's it's nearly impossible to do. If you think you're going to raise $50 million or $100 million and go out and hire people who've done it before to do TV online, you're going to fail.*[5]

Vice and Shane Smith may have counter-cultural feel and philosophy (his aim is to expose 'the absurdity of the modern condition'),[6] but Vice is both profitable and extremely well financed. Privately owned, since 2011 it has received $580 million in four funding rounds from three investors[7] (this is over four times the investments in BuzzFeed). According to industry watchers, this represents a company valuation of $2.5 billion. Its output is overwhelmingly video, and its YouTube channel has over 11 million subscribers and averages over 50 million video views every month. According to Bloomberg,[8] 2012 revenues were $175 million, estimated revenues for 2014 are $500 million, and for 2016 $1 billion.

Now based in Brooklyn (with a UK office in Shoreditch) it has around 400 employees in the US and bureaus in 36 countries.[9]

'Vice has a lot of money'

Vice's investors are not so much tech industry players as 'old media' companies who want to capitalise on its appeal to millennials. In 2011 it received $50 million from a consortium including WPP, Raine (a merchant bank backed by Hollywood and Silicon Valley), and Tom Freston, ex-CEO of Viacom. In 2013, 21st Century Fox acquired a 5% stake for $70 million. According to Smith, these funds were required for global expansion (and helped facilitate moves into India via 21st Century Fox's Star channels and into Europe via Sky):

> *Why? Because to be a global media brand takes a lot of money; connections with advertisers in all these countries is incredibly expensive.*[10]

The biggest funding deal came in 2014 when A&E Networks acquired 10% for $250 million. Despite these deals, and indeed due to these deals, the founders still have majority control of the board:[11]

> The reason we did the 21st Century deal was to keep control [...] We were offered $1.5 billion to sell during that process. We had pretty much every media company after us, but we got the deal I wanted.[12]

This is important to keep Vice Media competitive:

> They are big slow moving ships. They take a long time to turn around. They've got big questions to answer to their boards. That's something we didn't have until recently. That's a key thing for Vice. In spite of all our investment we are less than 30% owned by investors, so [effectively have] complete control of the board. (Interviewee)

'We have developed this weird, Willy Wonka fucking content factory'[13]

The span of Vice Media's operations are relatively complex to map. At the core of its activities is digital video. This represents around 80% of output, made up as follows:

- Vice.com, the main website that has versions in 24 languages. The huge array of content is organised into sections, including music, fashion, travel, sports, tech, food, NSFW (not safe for work), LBGT. *Vice* magazine, including back issues, can also be accessed.
- International news is a stand-alone division as of 2013, although its content can appear in sections of the main website also. Vice News is divided into beats, including politics, opinion and analysis, war and conflict, defence and security, crime and drugs, and also into regions – Americas, Middle East, Africa, Europe, Asia & Pacific. Vice News does not offer universal coverage, nor does it have to fit in with fixed structures like rolling coverage or scheduled bulletins. Vice News tends to make commitments to specific topics and stay with these long-term. It has made over 100 short films and several long-form documentaries about Ukraine. Syria is another focus point with reports from foreign Jihadists and Shi'a Militia (see

'Ghosts of Aleppo'). It has also prioritised thematic news strands – for example, 'Young and Gay', which has reported from 'Putin's Russia', Jamaica, and Belgrade. Vice News is one of the fastest growing channels on YouTube with over a million subscribers and over 250 million views since launch.[14]

- In addition there are online thematic video channels (also available in different languages). News is one such channel, and in addition there is Noisey (music, which also produces music video and hosts events), Motherboard (science/tech), The Creator's Project ('a global celebration of art and technology', part-funded by Intel), Fightland (mixed martial arts), and Thump (electronic music and culture).

- Vice Films (VBS.tv). This division produces documentaries and television shows. In 2008 it received plaudits for 'Heavy Metal in Baghdad', a documentary which followed the thrash metal band Acrassicauda in Iraq. Vice TV, a ten-episode documentary series, was produced for HBO in 2013. In addition there is a 24-hour terrestrial news service which blends live programming with documentaries and is broadcast in 18 countries. In March 2015 Vice and HBO announced a four-year content deal which will expand its presence on the HBO channel. The key elements of this were that the Vice weekly documentary series received a four-year extension and the number of episodes was increased to 35 from 14, HBO agreed to air 32 Vice 'specials' through to 2018, Vice will provide a daily 30-minute 'Vice' newscast for 48 weeks of the year, and the HBO Now broadband service will carry a Vice-branded channel.

Non-video activities include *Vice* magazine, which is now responsible for only around 5% of revenues,[15] Vice Books, Vice Records, 'The Old Blue Last' (a pub and live venue in Shoreditch where, to quote their website, 'Shakespeare, rent-boys, and thugs used to hang out') and last but not least, being a key element of their commercialisation strategy, Virtue, an ad agency (clients include Nike, Vodaphone Dell, and North Face).

'We went from a Gen X company as an indie mag to a Gen Y company online'[16]

Vice began as the *Voice of Montreal*, a job creation project for Haitian immigrants. In 1994 Shane Smith (who had been selling ads), Suroosh

Alvi and Gavin McInnes took the magazine over in what Smith freely admits were shady circumstances,[17] dropped the 'o' in the title, and created *Vice*, an underground music magazine given away free on the streets and in record stores. Smith was a talented publisher and succeeded in both selling ads and producing controversial content. *Vice* thrived and grew into self-proclaimed 'hipster bible'.

Viceland.com was launched 1996 (the name Vice.com was, at that time, unsurprisingly already taken). This marked Vice's start not only online but also with video, which was to become its centre of gravity. Smith was hungry for growth:

> We decided to go after our demographic – the cool kids in London or Berlin or Stockholm – and get scale that way.[18]

Vice relocated to Brooklyn, New York in 2001, where Smith's deal-making nous and flamboyant personality continued to spur growth. Vice's output of video guides – covering a medley of topics from sex to self-esteem – gained traction with new viewers and new advertisers.

A step change occurred in 2007 when a deal was made with Tom Freston, CEO of Viacom (owner of MTV), to create VBS.TV, an online video network – MTV would provide funding and Vice would supply content (Vice later bought the Viacom stake back for an undisclosed sum). In the same year Spike Jonze, renowned music video and film director (*Being John Malkovitch*) became Creative Director. (In 2011 Viceland.com and VBS.tv were combined into Vice.com.) When Google decided to finance companies and brands to create digital channels on YouTube, Vice was selected, receiving $100 million.[19]

Smith had identified the long-term potential of digital video early – although he initially assumed it would replace TV. Now Vice is more open-minded:

> In 2006 or so, Shane, to his credit, saw that the Hulus and the YouTubes of this world were building the infrastructure for video distribution, 'putting in the pipe' as he says, but at some point something was going to be needed to fill that pipe, and it can't all be cats dancing on pianos and UGC low rent content [... so] our push is all around premium content [...] the content you make for online should be as good as the content you make for TV. And for a long time our view was that 'TV's dead'. Five years ago we had slides with pictures of TVs with crosses through them,

and that was pretty naïve because TV's still pretty high, it's just proliferated, it's on different screens […] And so now we are embracing it and we view ourselves as platform agnostic. So it's about creating as much content for as many different destinations and media and platforms as possible, and whether that platform is your watch, Oculus Rift, or a linear TV channel, it's just about us working with the best partners, and creating formats fit for those spaces. (Interviewee)

'They are the only people who have worked out how to do video on the net efficiently'

The Vice tone is distinctive and raw – 'bad boy content […] edgy stuff from war zones, sex, drugs and violence'.[20] Vice's goal is to give audiences 'genuine' stories about topics that interest them, in their language, and made by them (the average age of journalists is 25):[21]

Every five years we give over the company to the interns. Young people have been marketed to since they were babies because cartoons were made to sell cereal. So they have the most sophisticated bullshit detectors of all time. And the only way to circumnavigate that bullshit detector is to not bullshit. And what that means is that young people have to shoot it, young people have to cut it, it has to be made by them.[22]

If Vice content is platform agnostic, then it needs to be designed to travel, to be able to migrate from web to mobile to terrestrial TV. This governs how footage is produced:

Every single space that's available is an edit suite. We cut for mobile, we cut for online, we cut for TV and for features, so we re-cut and re-cut and re-cut, and we have to own that process, and we shoot thinking that way, too, modularly.[23]

And this mandates high production values:

A lot of time it's a lottery […] I don't think you can bank on winning the lottery. You have to say, 'How can I grow my video business every day?' And that's quality. That's the only answer.[24]

Many platforms mean more opportunities for revenue generation:

Vice in particular are incredibly sophisticated about thinking about all of the different ways or all of the platforms on which their content, their videos in particular, can exist and how it can be sold in all of those different platforms. (Competitor)

There are however no ambitions to metamorphose into a high-growth tech company. If anything Vice is moving back into legacy territory:

We know what we want to do, broadly speaking, to be the biggest youth media company in the world, that is a publisher not a technology business. We are not a technology business, we are a content and distribution business. It's about making the quality as good as you can, for as many places as you can, and distributing it as broadly as you can, to as many eyeballs as you can. We want to staff up and get better at the technology side of things [...] but it all loops back to getting people to view and watch your content.[25]

'We are with John McAfee right now, suckers'[26]

The thing is: Dennis Rodman is absurd. North Korea is absurd. And our whole mission statement at Vice is the absurdity of the modern condition. So it made perfect sense for us.[27]

Smith likes stories that 'punch you in the face'.[28] An on-screen correspondent introduces 'Heavy Metal in Baghdad' by describing it as 'risky, dangerous, and fucking stupid'. This neatly summarises the Vice approach:

They have done some amazing journalism. Don't get me wrong. They've produced stories that no one else has been able to produce. And it's partly because they have a lot of money and are willing to take a lot of risks. Some would say stupid risks. They have sent reporters out to really, really dangerous places and then just kind of crossed their fingers and hoped that nothing happens. But they have got some really great stuff and they have really pushed the boundary. (Competitor)

Vice News favours gritty on-the-ground reporting from hard-to-reach and sometimes dangerous hotspots, as well as hard-hitting domestic stories. It practises 'immersive journalism', meaning journalists involve themselves in the situation and the story as it develops. While far from standard J-school practice, the results can be compelling. The Creator's Project experimented with using virtual reality technology to place the viewer into a virtual recreation of the case of a Mexican migrant who was beaten and tasered to death by US border patrol agents in 2010.

'Gonzo' is an adjective regularly applied to Vice's journalism. It derives from 'gonzo journalism', an approach that blends experience and fiction and was popularised by Hunter S. Thompson (Smith was given a signed first edition of *Fear and Loathing in Las Vegas* by his father[29]). Two gonzo scoops in particular brought Vice notoriety within the news industry, and to the attention of a much wider public.

The first involved internet millionaire John McAfee, who was on the run in Belize after being sought for questioning in connection over the death of his neighbour. When he surfaced with an 18-year-old girlfriend he was accompanied by two Vice reporters who were documenting events. Wired commented:

> *Vice directly contributed to McAfee's capture by revealing his location in the metadata of a photo it published. This was deeply stupid. People have been pointing out the dangers of inadvertently leaving GPS tags in cellphone pictures for years and years. Vice is the same publication that regularly drops in on revolutions and all manner of criminals. They should have known better. Then, it followed up this egregiously stupid action with a far worse one. Vice photographer Robert King apparently lied on his Facebook page and Twitter in order to protect McAfee. Like McAfee, he claimed that the geodata in the photo had been manipulated to conceal their true location.[30]*

Vice's response summarises its culture (unapologetic) and its news philosophy (expose absurdity):

> *Our team has just returned home to debrief and deliver said footage. We have always been transparent in our film-making and will continue that practice – this will be no exception. If we fucked up, you can be sure it will be in the film, which we will show everyone, everywhere – warts and all. The story as a whole has engaged people around the world precisely because it is so freaky, and even if it shows that we made mistakes on the ground during a very hectic and dangerous week of reporting on McAfee's mistakes, we are sure it's going to make one hell of a documentary.[31]*

A second gonzo scoop from North Korea engendered criticism from politicians as well as industry peers. As part of its HBO documentary series, Vice correspondent Ryan Duffy, Dennis Rodman, and the Harlem Globetrotters visited North Korea where they played a basketball game with the national team and met Kim Jong-un. Vice was charged with supporting a regime responsible for horrendous human rights violations. Smith was unchastened:

> We didn't go over there to stop a geopolitical crisis [...] get them to disarm their nuclear program. We went over to open up any sort of dialogue, which we don't have. And we did that. I think that's a success. We're not trying to be Jesus Christ and solve the world's problems. We were trying to film a documentary. And that's what we did.[32]

'The news stuff. That's what's driving me'[33]

> We were an entertainment brand, and then as we expanded around the world we realised that there were these serious problems and I said 'Why isn't anyone saying anything about this, where are the adults?' and I realised I had the biggest platform for youth in the world, so I will start saying something about it, so we started doing news. And we weren't perfect, but our audience said 'yes' [...] and that's been the fastest part of our business ever since.[34]

The North Korea report led to a reputation for being 'more jackass than journalism',[35] but Smith and Vice are serious about news:

> Our audience is actually saying make more news. We tell stories that a lot of other people don't tell, and we tell them in a different way. That's what's really been resonating with our audience. So we're going to double down.[36]

> We thought it would be the traditional areas of youth culture that would get traction [...] but it was the current affairs stuff which was resonating, so particularly in the US, where you see TV news consumption just drop off, it wasn't that people weren't interested in news, they weren't being communicated to in a language they understand by people of their generation.[37]

Vice is also serious about serious news:

Long form, I believe, is [viable] for the first time ever, because of bandwidth, because of young people consuming TV-length content online or through mobile or tablets. Gen Y people now consume whole movies online, so 20 minutes, 30 minutes, 40 minutes isn't too long. We're in the right place at the right time.[38]

'The Islamic State', a five-part documentary made by Vice News with the help of Medyan Dairieh, a freelance journalist, inside Islamic State-controlled areas of Syria, is perhaps Vice's best known foray into long-form serious news, winning the network respect and over 20 million YouTube video views.

Vice News is only just over a year old. It was born in the social media era, where individuals live tweet and film events as they unfold on their smartphones. This reality shapes its approach. Vice shuns the 'middle aged talking to the middle aged' or 'young correspondents voicing words written by someone over 50' (interviewee) and instead relies on reports from young multicultural correspondents who find their own stories and tell them in their own words. This avoids the 'tunnel vision of the news rooms, where everyone is looking at what the others are doing':

The problem with the news cycle today and the news media in general is that it's kindergarten playing soccer. The ball goes over here, and everyone goes here. The ball goes over there, and everyone goes there.[39]

As news becomes more central, investments are increasing:

So we have had to up the ante massively in that area over the past few years [...] when we started that stuff it would be Shane going to Liberia, and we didn't have the big insurance premiums of CNN or the BBC, he was kind of taking it on himself. It's a bit different when you have other people doing it [...] one of our correspondents from the Ukraine got taken hostage, happily he was freed, but that could have turned pretty bad [...] that's a big shift [...] we were the snarky upstarts for a long time, but now news is actually a pretty serious thing. (Interviewee)

In 2013 Vice Media launched a 12-part news magazine programme for HBO. Described on the show's website as tackling 'global issues often overlooked by traditional media', the series won Vice an Emmy in 2014 and a third series is in production:

Their first foray into television, they win an Emmy on HBO which is sort of the premier TV outlet in the United States. I can tell you there are production companies in the TV business have been doing it for 30 years and never even been nominated for an Emmy. That's not luck. They are completely focused on their creative product.[40]

The series represented another step change in Vice's attitude to news:

Before we could just go in and immerse ourselves in the story [...] This time, we wanted to give people more context. So we learned a lot on what works and what doesn't for a 15 minute format. The stories had to be better. We couldn't go to a country and come back with a B-minus.[41]

'Is Vice profitable? Very'

We have a rule that everything that we do has to make money. We are growing at 100% a year without our big windfall deals that we are going to be announcing in Q4 or early Q1. We're getting quite big, for us at least, in the dollars sense.[42]

Vice's content is free, underwritten by deals with commercial partners that range from branded channels to branded content:

We're lucky in that we work with some of the world's biggest brands, and our capacity to sell outstrips our capacity to scale. We do things differently [...] what you can do is start making innovative deals at the brand level. A lot of online content companies fail because they don't go directly to the brand, they don't make unique or creative monetization deals.[43]

Branded online content is viewed as continuation of an accepted industry practice:

We are absolutely reliant on our brand partners [...] brand money enables us to make the work we want to make, and we try to make it as compelling a proposition as we can for the brand partners [...] The model on our dotcom and our own channels is to create programming that is editorially sound, and we push out editorially, and the brands can sponsor that content [...] When you break it down our model is still reasonably traditional. It's still traditional media formats and it's creating programming

*that we work with brands to sponsor [...] so the monetisation model at its
core is not particularly new, I just guess we are doing it better than others.*[44]

(However, there have been claims that Vice allows brands to influence
journalistic content,[45] and that stories have been dropped because of
potential conflicts with advertisers and brand partners.[46])

It's a Vice credo that standard mass media advertising messages do
not work for millennials and younger audiences:

> *Gen Y, Gen X, Millennials, however you want to segment them, broadly
> 18–24s, have been marketed to since they were newborns, so they have
> sophisticated bullshit detectors, so the only way that you circumvent that
> is to not bullshit, so tell stories that are authentic and compelling, and do
> it with brand partners, but when you are making video, for example,
> don't litter it with product messages because it's just going to act as a
> barrier to success. (Interviewee)*

Millennials respond to 'the joy of not being sold anything'. Advertisers
therefore need to adjust their role – they must think like content creators,
not marketers. If they can produce branded content that entertains
millennials, they can turn them into fans.

> *Our view on this hasn't changed over the last five years. Brands should act
> like modern media companies, must have an editorial tone of voice,
> should have this sustained communication with their audience and not
> treat them like idiots. And the number one rule is to make entertainment
> not advertising. Make something that people genuinely want to watch.
> Advertising is very interruptive. Our model is to make something of
> cultural value and give something back.*[47]

The Vice model makes brands into media organisations (or publishers,
perhaps). This is becoming common practice, but does not always work:

> *Brands have become the commissioners of the modern day. But there's been
> this content explosion, and every brand thinks that it has to have a content
> strategy, and that's just led to a lot of rubbish. A lot of brand directors and
> marketing directors now think that they have to do something in the content
> space that isn't a TV ad [but] actually all they know how to do and how
> their agencies know how to do is make TV ads. So it's a challenge for the
> brands. It's certainly a challenge for the big creative agencies. TV still gets a*

lot of money but they know that times are changing and there's more money being spent on this area so they have to have a play in this space, but they don't really know how to make engaging content for online. (Interviewee)

Virtue, Vice's advertising agency,[48] devises content strategies and campaigns for brand partners. Vice then creates content and distributes it on its media platforms. 'AdVice', an ad network, then 'activates' the content through the Vice sites and on social media.

This recasting of brands as media companies undermines the role of the ad agency:

Most of the brands that we work with are moving away from spots or traditional advertising and they want to move more into sponsorships, production partnerships, they want to go direct, they don't want to go through agencies any more. (Interviewee)

Branded content is not, however, the only revenue source. Vice retains the intellectual property in most of the content it produces, and generates additional revenues by licensing material for mobile, film, and TV internationally:

Most companies concentrate on one form of revenue in one country. But we concentrate on five forms of revenue in about 50 countries, which is fine for us. We'll take it.[49]

Deal-making skills

Vice is valuable to its commercial partners because it has mastered two things other media companies are weak at: how to link advertising with online video and how to capture the attention of 18–34-year-olds who watch little or no television. Shane Smith's great skill is how to capture value from these two capabilities:

The basic message is: 'We're going to make content that young people are going to enjoy, and it is going to help your brand.' Then we make that content. We exploit that content. We have a TV show in China, we have mobile in India, we license it to TV in 23 countries in the world, we create a YouTube channel. It drives subscriptions, and it drives millions of video views. Intel is happy because they are getting more ads at more scale globally. We get paid for the content before we ever put it on YouTube. Those are the types of deals that you have to make. Brands want scale. They want engagement. If you just wait for somebody else to make money for you, I don't believe that's going to happen.[50]

Deal-making is one of Vice's – or Smith's – core areas of innovation. A series of deals stretching back to the initial acquisition of the *Voice of Montreal* shaped Vice's development. The YouTube deal, which allowed Vice to scale up production, has been promoted by YouTube on television and in the press, further boosting Vice's visibility:

We were making [...] content for YouTube, they were paying us to make premium channels, there was a big investment from them, $100 million [...] to turn YouTube from a UCG platform into something that could compete [...] and we have done well out of that, they love us because we have really high engagement rates; people watch for a long time. (Interviewee)

Similarly, The Creators Project, a partnership with Intel to 'push the boundaries of creative expression', brings revenue, content, and reputation:

The Creators Project is the gold standard. It's a big, big thing. It's been in existence for five years now [...] It houses a huge amount of content with some of the world's most celebrated artists and musicians [...] Last year the experiential part of it had 720,000 event attendees on five continents, 40 staff work on it in the US, they spend $20 million dollars a year on it, $40 million at its peak. (Interviewee)

Vice grows through its deals, and they are many. It has a deal with Facebook to produce customised campaigns for advertisers, a partnership with Twitter to produce a daily news show composed of one-minute clips, a joint venture with Antenna in Greece, and a production deal with Youku, the largest video site in China.[51]

A unique voice and excellently positioned for growth

Vice is an old media–new media hybrid. Its content is pretty traditional – hard-hitting news reportage – but distributed on new digital platforms, and produced in a social media 'millennial' style. Its tone is challenging and alternative, but its growth rests on good old-fashioned deal-making with advertisers, distributors, and established players looking for growth.

The tremendous coherence between Vice's culture, product, tone, and strategy stems directly from Shane Smith. His organisation is excellently positioned for growth – it has a unique 'voice' that is hard to imitate, generates multiple revenue streams, and appears to hold the key to attracting a young demographic that legacy media feel increasingly unable to reach. Its true innovation perhaps lies in its ability to take traditional sources of competitive advantage from old media and shape them into an organisation that can compete in the emerging digital world.

7

Conclusions – So Why *are* Some Digital News Organisations More Successful?

Exchange between Jonah Peretti and Shane Smith:[1]

Peretti: Don't you find that [...] mainstream media [...] come to Vice and say 'OK, we need to figure this out and we can't, so we want to buy you?'

Smith: Yes, I have noticed that [...] and part of the problem is that it wouldn't even save them if they bought us [...] staying independent allows us to do a lot of things that we wouldn't be able to do otherwise [...] even if they bought us they would still have a massive legacy industrial media beast that they have to feed.

Uncovering the pattern

This concluding chapter sifts through the detail of the case studies in search of factors common to these organisations that might contribute to their success with digital news. Over-simplification is a danger. Any universal prescription developed from a set of heterogeneous and idiosyncratic case studies is unlikely to be very effective.

Yet a common constellation of factors can be detected in these companies, and it is worth discussing these, and their implications for organisations which are behind them on the innovation path. What follows, therefore, is not a recipe for creating a digital news organisation, but a discussion of the factors that the case study organisations have in common – to varying degrees.

This pattern is not complex – many elements are standard practice for high-performing organisations. Others, however, are specific to the emerging digital news industry and to the nature of competition and consumption within it. Some are relatively straightforward to replicate (although they may require significant resource commitments); others are, unfortunately, in the jargon of core competence literature, 'non-imitable' – that is, they generally cannot be acquired by organisations if they do not have them already. So here is the list.

Element 1: A sureness and singularity of purpose

All of the organisations profiled in this book display a direct and powerful shared sense of purpose. They know what they are trying to do, which audiences they serve, and how to create value for them.

This singularity of purpose is more or less what management texts call vision, but it is more clearly defined, and acts as a more specific call to action. It is embedded in the company's DNA and expressed in many facets of the organisation (Quartz is probably the best example of this). It functions as a heuristic, speeding decision-making and ensuring that energies are focused on the same goal. It blends into and provides the bedrock for the organisation's strategy.

Element 2: Unequivocal strategic focus

> *The ability to articulate a strategic focus and singularity of purpose, despite the messiness underneath of what's actually changing in the marketplace and within your own company, I feel, is part of what sets these high quality players apart. (Interviewee)*

In addition to an extremely singular vision for their organisation, the companies profiled here have a clearly defined strategic focus that almost functions as an internal protocol governing decision-making. In addition, both strategy and focus in these leading players were coherent – the strategy unfolds from the vision and is embedded in it.

The strategies themselves were relatively simple (e.g. the *Guardian*'s decision to go free, go global, and go open, and get profile through big investigative campaigns, or BuzzFeed's forensic focus on decoding and exploiting the keys to virality). In fast-moving environments strategy needs to be very straightforward – otherwise it risks being pushed to one side, or even undermining growth because it strays over too wide an area.

This combination of a powerful, intuitive vision embedded in a clear organisational strategy brings many benefits:

Clarity in an extremely volatile environment

For news media, the industry is changing extremely fast. Planning horizons have contracted – the five-, ten-, or even 15-year forecasts that underpin traditional approaches to strategy are neither feasible nor useful. Larger organisations with complicated strategies, especially legacy ones that need a strategy to cover both old and new activities, risk getting lost in complex plans that are based on assumptions about the future that are really just guesswork. A simple strategy, one that chimes coherently with the overall vision, avoids the strategic inconsistencies, *volte faces,* and inertia that have been evident in the digital strategies developed by many legacy news organisations.

Sets priorities, establishes boundaries, avoids distractions

Clarity improves decision-making and ensures intelligent resource commitment. This type of strategy defines 'this is what we do, and this is what we do not do'. It allows organisations to be discriminating. Boundaries are clear, and decision-making simplified at all levels of the organisation. Employees can work more autonomously. Simplicity also means ill-judged decisions are more evident sooner, and easier to correct. The clarity of these strategies focuses organisational energies and improves the manner in which resources are deployed: specifically it prevents resources from being invested in non-core areas. BuzzFeed is enviably well financed, and generates strong digital revenues. It could follow a very exploratory strategy. Yet Peretti has insisted that the organisation must not be distracted by tempting opportunities outside its defined sphere (for example, no white-label products, no paywall, no legacy-style TV products).

Brings agility and consistency, allows course correction

Strategies that are straightforward and easily grasped speed decision-making. This in turn increases organisational agility. A relatively simple strategy embedded in a widely held singularity of purpose brings coherence and consistency. Simplicity also creates wiggle room, the latitude to change and experiment. So organisations can change course relatively painlessly – they are not (yet, perhaps), to use a Vice interviewee's metaphor, big slow-moving ships that take a long time to turn around. Rather, they can accommodate, evolve, grow, and experiment in step with the market.

Clarifies target market and value proposition

These visions capture, in the words of one interviewee, 'the one function you have to perform better than all the others'. In the terms of management theory, they embody a differentiated market position and value proposition for that market. In Clayton Christensen's words they define 'the job that has to be done' for a particular audience group. This is necessary because it allows prioritisation of attention and of resource investment. It also allows sophisticated metrics to be developed that measure performance in critical areas.

Element 3: Strong leadership

An exceptional set of individuals are in charge of these organisations, individuals who are capable of developing a genuinely original vision and strategy, and then influencing others to work together to achieve it.

Of all the success factors discussed in this chapter, smart, compelling leadership is first among equals. It is a rare commodity and very hard for companies with weaker, less decisive leaders to compete against. Common characteristics of these leaders include the following:

- They have worked out a way forward. Many senior figures in the media, especially legacy media, lack a coherent sense of how their industry is developing, or of the forces that are shaping the strategic context and how to respond to them. As a result they lack a truly compelling competitive vision. The leaders here are strategists *and* figureheads. They have deciphered the strategic environment in a way that makes sense to them, their staff, and key stakeholders and divined either an opportunity or a way forward in it. They are alert and environmentally attuned enough to be able to redefine the problem they are solving for their audiences, as the strategic environment evolves.
- These leaders understand the ascendancy of tech in the media and respect tech skills as much as they do journalistic ones. This is not a simple skill combination to achieve – digital and technology expertise

are to some extent in opposition (few people have a natural affinity with words *and* numbers), and many journalists have yet to appreciate the centrality of technology in the media.

- They are extremely skilled communicators. News organisations have challenging workforces – it is a journalist's job to be articulate, to be critical, to question those in authority. Such a workforce can erect formidable cultural blocks to digital transition, especially when the path of digital media evolution is uncertain. These leaders have been able to get staff to buy into their vision, even to accept changes that may not be in their own interests.

Element 4: Pro-digital culture

The battle now is between people who think this is a problem, and people who think this is an exciting opportunity. (Interviewee)

All the organisations profiled here have strong cultures. For the clean sheet organisations they are resolutely pro-digital cultures also. Digital is seen as an opportunity: a battle, but one that can be won:

There is a really interesting element between innovation and legacy [...] people who are innovating, they see everything as an opportunity. It's not digital-only focus. They don't view challenges as bad things, they are just purely focused on opportunity. It's a mindset. It's not a digital culture and it's not a youth culture [...] it's a culture where everything is viewed as an opportunity, everything [...] It's exciting, it's a problem to figure out. (Interviewee)

Legacy players' cultures are partially pro-digital – but critically their leaders and some opinion formers (not always the same individuals) do 'get' digital. They understand the broad trajectory of their industry and as a result comprehend the importance of digital technologies and data analytics, and are open to thinking about what constitutes quality journalism in the digital domain, especially in mobile/social environments.

Pockets of digital obduracy can persist. Symptoms tend to be nostalgia for the pre-internet era, snide comments about cat videos, and, most perniciously, an assumption that online is negatively correlated with quality. The obstinacy of these attitudes may also stem from a personal sense of threat. The digital world is a young world, and prizes a different set of skills. The value of decades of experience and great contacts has shrunk in relation to an affinity for technology and instant social media postings from those witnessing breaking news as it happens. The result is that different layers of culture can exist within a single organisation:

> If you drew the organogram, there's a layer that's very vested and it's controlled and it's staying the same. This is the layer of ice, and there's fish under there. It's all going to be fine, we just have to perforate it and it will go. It's not deep resistance, but it's enough. (Interviewee)

Cultural rigidity can cause digital talent to exit legacy players. Here is Ezra Klein's explanation for leaving the *Washington Post* to start Vox: 'We were badly held back not just by the technology, but by the culture of journalism.'[2] More broadly, cultural rigidity can lead to a systemic inability to seize the potential of emerging digital markets. It is notable that, with a few exceptions, the foundations of the digital news industry are being laid by new players, some of whom did not initially look like news organisations, but are increasingly morphing into them. C. W. Anderson's investigation into the demise of the US regional newspapers in the face of digital technologies finds culture a leading culprit:

> Local journalism's occupational self-image, its vision of itself as an autonomous workforce conducting original reporting on behalf of a unitary public, blocked the kind of cross-institutional collaboration that might have helped journalism thrive in an era of fractured communication. This failure, in turn, highlights the central normative problem [...] Local journalism's vision of itself – as an institutionally grounded profession that empirically informs (and even, perhaps, 'assembles') the public – is a noble vision of tremendous democratic importance. But the unreflexive commitment to a particular and historically contingent version of this self-image now undermines these larger democratic aspirations.[3]

Even without outright cultural conflicts, there are opportunity costs when a single organisation is required to build a digital business while simultaneously transforming a legacy one:

> There's a lot of head scratching going on about all of this. What happens is you find yourself oscillating between, 'let's just think of how we can do

this digitally', and then 'we can't think about how we do things digitally until we sort out print'. And if you obsess about the role of print you become incredibly inwardly focused and process focused when really you should be thinking about what is going on in the digital world. The whole thing about Quartz is that they don't need to think about any of these things. (Interviewee)

A strong culture can always be traced back to a strong leader. An authentic commitment to and respect for a leader and his or her vision accelerates the adoption of strategy and eliminates cultural obstacles. Insights into how this dynamic operates come from Molly Graham (incidentally, the daughter of the *Washington Post*'s Don Graham) in an account of her time in charge of 'culture branding' at Facebook:

A founder saying something is like throwing a rock into a pond and watching the ripples. People immediately start repeating it. At Facebook, Mark [Zuckerberg] would say something and the next day it would be on the walls.[4]

Cultural obstacles will abate anyway as digital becomes the norm, and workforces renew themselves. Newer generations of digital journalists synthesise tech and journalism naturally:

We have some editorial interns, and what's been fascinating is [...] the natural friendships and relationships that they have built with our younger engineers [...] these people hang out together, they drink together, they come up with ideas together [...] they have just gravitated towards each other, because these young sparky developers are working here because of the content, and the young twenty-something journalists joining, they have only ever lived in an online world, so to them technology is a tool for their storytelling, it's natural. You see it all over the place, just meeting, talking even though they are in different departments. People like me are from the Cold War era. It's a natural thing, it's just happening. (Interviewee)

Fluid approach to what content is, to what constitutes quality in news

In some ways the Guardian and the New York Times are trying to find out what BuzzFeed has and [...] tack that on. And I don't mean listicles

> *[...] what I mean is a structure, a process, a mindset that supports a digital focus. (Interviewee)*

A pro-digital culture dissolves preconceptions about what constitutes quality news and how stories should be presented. Legacy players have struggled from the start with the fact that the format protocols developed over centuries for print news do not really translate to digital devices, or at least only sub-optimally, and often fail to take advantage of the potential of the new medium for storytelling. This leaves their content vulnerable to disruption by new players who do exploit the new functionalities.

The new players view content as a fluid entity – a story can take whatever form will best convey its message, or that will ensure most people read it. While the act of storytelling remains constant, the default architecture for that story, how it is told, which media are used, changes.

Entirely new formats have emerged – notably the listicle and the quiz. The *New York Times* masthead culture may be sniffy about these, but its own most popular story for 2013 was a quiz that would fit perfectly on BuzzFeed ('How Y'all, Youse and You Guys Talk'). As Robinson Meyer pointed out,[5]

> *Think about that. A news app, a piece of software about the news made by in-house developers, generated more clicks than any article. And it did this in a tiny amount of time. The app only came out on December 21, 2013. That means that in [the] days it was online in 2013, it generated more visits than any other piece.*

Element 5: Deep integration of tech and journalism, because 'the future of the news is written in code'

> *What the leaders in digital news understand is that success depends on the connection between mobile, social, design, workflow and CMS.[6]*

Journalism and technology are integrated in digital natives. Legacy print organisations know they need to mesh these areas, but find this proposition challenging, requiring as it does changes to all kinds of structures and hierarchies ranging from the physical (office layouts) to the virtual (reporting relationships and cultural values).

The *New York Times* Innovation report noted that its technology and editorial departments communicated poorly, and more significantly that the two were not even meant to communicate. The degree to which these areas are integrated is a clear point of differentiation between clean sheet and legacy players:

> With the old economics destroyed, organizational forms perfected for industrial production have to be replaced with structures optimized for digital data. It makes increasingly less sense even to talk about a publishing industry, because the core problem publishing solves – the incredible difficulty, complexity, and expense of making something available to the public – has stopped being a problem.[7]

Physical proximity is an obvious manifestation of this issue. In digital natives, digital, tech, and often commercial teams too, sit close together. But increasingly tech and journalistic skills are synthesised at an individual level. This can happen naturally through exposure to the technology systems, or through recruitment and training – at Quartz, for example, many journalists have some degree of coding knowledge.

Failure to combine these fields well can cause key staff to exit. Ezra Klein also left the *Washington Post* to join Vox partly because of content management systems. Vox had Chorus, and the *Washington Post* did not. (Chorus allows journalists to create and publish content intuitively, but also to share it on social sites, interact with users, while generating data that allows performance and engagement to be analysed and content optimised.)

Social and mobile – not an afterthought

> If Facebook's algorithm smiles on a publisher, the rewards, in terms of traffic, can be enormous.[8]

Blending digital tech and editorial alters the shape of journalism, even more so as social becomes increasingly important as a distribution platform for news.

> Taken together, you have your workflow and CMS enabling your design to maximise your social sharing, which leads to more traffic, which leads to more sharing, thus creating a virtuous circle of delicious audience-growing goodness.[9]

An increasing number of readers (e.g. for the *Washington Post* this figure is already over 50%[10]) reach digital news sites through social media and algorithm-driven search engines. Many of these consumers are millennials, a market that is particularly attractive to advertisers, and notoriously reluctant to consume media content in traditional mass media formats.

If social-mobile is the growth field, then the purveyors of digital news need to ensure that their content is not only present on those platforms, but presented in a way to maximise consumption and sharing:

Legacy players can mistake formality for sophistication. The pretentions that are built into formality don't work on the web. (Interviewee)

A further challenge is that the technological advantages evaporate fast, the result of the pace of innovation in digital markets. Even Vox's CMS, currently a huge asset, will need updating in the mid-term:

The pace of technology is such that anything you build turns out to have been the wrong approach five years later. The longer you've been around, the longer you've had technology systems, the more legacy crap you will have to deal with [...] it's always legacy and it's always changing dramatically fast [...] it becomes legacy in three years. So who has the advantage when technology is so critical to everything? It's the companies who can afford to be continually ripping out and changing the infrastructure, not just to their companies, but to everyone else's companies, and that's Amazon, Google, not yet Facebook but I wouldn't be surprised if they go there. (Interviewee)

Then add commerce

A further dimension of melding is combining sales and marketing activities with editorial ones. This is a tricky area, but there is an intrinsic interdependence between content creation and revenue generation, and some forward-looking digital news organisations, rather than erecting Chinese walls, actively blend these areas. (Interviewee)

So journalism and tech need to blend. Increasingly, commercial elements need to be added to the mix also:

This bit's really key, the bit around the journalism, tech, commerce blended [...] I think that's the next big thing because if those things aren't working there's only so much you can do around the product, around the design, to make it better or to drive engagement. We are fundamentally a content product. People come to the Guardian for its journalism, so it is how those two bits work together that will really define the next couple of years. (Interviewee)

This aspect of digital publishing is developing fast:

It's really cranking up not only about big data and how you find insight in that but how the commerce works around news sites or online sites. It's changing really rapidly. (Interviewee)

This is an uncomfortable issue for legacy actors, transgressing as it does a fundamental tenet of quality journalism, the Chinese wall between editorial and commercial activities. This tenet can also be seen as the by-product of the sector's historically solid revenues:

Underlying that is a mentality that existed at a time when newsrooms could afford, literally and figuratively, to exist in this magic bubble as if they had no connection to the business. (Interviewee)

Chinese walls are being punctured in many legacy publications:

Strong Chinese walls make cooperation between editorial and commercial divisions more difficult. There are good reasons to keep them apart. But the shift to digital means that in a range of areas (technology, analytics, new product development, developing new ways to monetise content that everyone is happy with, etc.) there is a growing need for cooperation and collaboration. So how do you do that, while retaining the division in areas where it is still needed? You need specific holes in the Chinese wall, and rules about what gets passed back and forth. Start-ups avoid this problem by having big chunks of the organisation (e.g. technology) report to editorial. (Interviewee)

All the cases here are actively pursuing native advertising. Sales teams are embedded in new products from the outset at the *Washington Post*:

The number one goal is to have embedded designers and engineers in the sales team. They have a very strong voice in the design of any product we are trying to develop.[11]

It is unlikely that this trend will reverse itself. Many expect online ad rates to decline further. This will exacerbate a search for scale – to grow digital audiences as quickly as possible to be in the best possible shape when ad rates collapse. It will also fuel the shift towards native, in turn accelerating the melding of tech, journalism, and sales activities:

> *The more bespoke it is, the less it's likely to be commoditised. The more we can say, 'We are building you a very special audience', the more we can defy the trend for ad rates to be driven into the ground. BuzzFeed and Vice are advertising agencies. (Interviewee)*

Further developments will concern a shift towards measuring attention:

> *Even up to a year ago it was 'we sell advertising on the website and you get paid around how many pages are served'. And a lot of those ads were never seen because they were at the bottom of a page but you still get paid for them. Whereas now, the technology that's coming through [...] is now about whether the ad is actually seen [...] If you are in your browser, it's pretty straightforward technology now to say, we know that this part of the page is being seen, so that data is being passed back (Interviewee)*

Talent is chasing the new ventures

> *The trends in American journalism are now clear: you will all spend the first year of your career begging us to give you a job. We will then spend the next few years of your career begging you not to set up your own start-up.*[12]

The blending of tech, journalism, and a commercial awareness needs to happen at an individual level, and digital news organisations require digital editorial thinkers – individuals who combine a mastery of journalism with an understanding of tech. Those who possess such a synthesis are in demand. If a digital news venture succeeds, the architects of that success will have money 'poured on to them' (interviewee) by competitors new and old:

> *We are in a bubbly time. Talent is chasing the new ventures, and talent floods to them. (Interviewee)*

Digital innovators will usually be able to earn far more from new players than from legacy companies. They will probably be given more autonomy (and perhaps stock options), and will not have to contend with the constrictions of legacy systems, processes, and culture. Legacy media are no longer automatically the employer of choice for talented staff, and they will need to have momentum if they are to keep the talent they have:

> *If you get this right you become a talent magnet. If you don't polarity reverses, and you can lose important people – Ezra Klein is a case in point. Human resource management, never a very high-priority concern, is now becoming strategically very important. (Interviewee)*

Element 6: Autonomous or decoupled

> *I'd speak at big newspaper industry conferences and say, 'you have to have a separate group.' And they would say, 'No you don't. We've got journalists. They are smart. We've got sales people. They know the market. Why duplicate the cost structure?' And I'd say, 'Go for it. Maybe you are different from everyone else. But the last 50 people who jumped off that cliff all died. So, you know, I'm going to go with gravity here. But maybe you can defy it.'[13]*

'Integrate or separate?' is a fundamental question for legacy organisations responding to disruptive innovation. As the quote from Clark Gilbert (CEO of Deseret News Publishing Company and ex-Harvard Business School professor who worked with Clayton Christensen on his theories of disruptive innovation) indicates, the scientific evidence is pretty clear that separation brings a higher likelihood of success. That is not to say that an internal unit will not work, but the odds for success are slimmer, and any success gained will be slower and more agonising than would have been the case had new businesses been created. Legacy players have a far larger management task than the clean sheet digital news organisations:

> *I don't think our problem is not knowing what to do digitally, or what to do with print. The problem is actually about the management of change. (Interviewee)*

Just as digital innovation has created a highly strategic human resource challenge, namely ensuring the availability of digital talent, so too has it made choices concerning the often prosaic issue of organisational structure highly tactical. Independence and autonomy clearly make life easier in volatile fast-moving industries. Autonomy allows organisations to grow and evolve in step with the market.

Vice and BuzzFeed are independent businesses under the stewardship of smart and compelling leaders who have a clear vision of where they want to take their organisations. Quartz is a stand-alone venture backed by Atlantic Media, again with very strong leadership that has a sophisticated and clearly articulated 'formula' for how it wants to move forward.

Outside the cases in this book, there are other examples in digital media where autonomy from the legacy parent seems to be positively correlated with success. The Mail Online operates with a high degree of autonomy from its print parent. In 2003, Schibsted, the consistently innovative Norwegian media group, set up a new unit to disrupt the advertising sales activities of its newspaper properties. Perhaps in recognition of this, recently, Forbes Inc., *Die Zeit*, and the *Dallas Morning News* have all adopted this strategy. The *Guardian* and *New York Times* have not taken this step, and both are performing well. But the question is, how much better would they have performed had the digital news units been autonomous?

It's far easier to launch a Quartz, a Vox, a FiveThirtyEight, or a Business Insider – with far fewer people and have them work together [...] people work better [...] in groups of a dozen or less, with streamlined decision-making. The Times' bigness – a huge asset in its reporting and its brand's institutional heft – is a handicap here, a consequence of basic human nature.[14]

A legacy organisation is actually trying not just to innovate, it is also trying to manage a mature business for cash flow; those two things are very different tasks that are best done by very different types of people. They both have to happen. (Interviewee)

Interviewees from legacy firms spoke of the difficulties arising from the need to 'keep reinventing and stripping out', 'constantly shifting and avoiding a steady state structure', and 'building liberated teams who own stuff and go end to end'. And should a legacy news organisation manage to build a new autonomous digital business that succeeds, what happens then?

I think the tricky part is that it's fairly easy for organisations that can be autonomous or decoupled. And the bit that I do not think that we have seen happen so far, and so it's an open question if it will happen ever, is, can an autonomous or decoupled part of a bigger news organisation then either take over or come back in and somehow change the bigger organisation? (Interviewee)

Element 7: Start early

There are important things around speed of travel. Everybody is heading in the same direction, and almost everyone in this area is portraying themselves as quite radical; we are not too sure what is over the horizon ahead of us, but we are heading for that horizon as fast as we can. (Interviewee)

Timing matters. An early start is a classic non-inimitable strategic advantage. Many quality news organisations have elegant and intelligent digital strategies *now*, but they started too late. Windows of opportunity have closed. They have yielded competitive territory which logically should have been theirs to new players.

Digital technologies have proved to be what Andrew Grove and Robert Burgelman in *Strategic Dynamics: Three Key Themes*[15] term a 'strategic inflection point' for legacy media industry. The basis of industry competition has changed, strategic assets (production and distribution systems, competencies and expertise) have lost their shine, or even become liabilities. Legacy media organisations find themselves in the 'valley of death' – they must either cross the valley (and undertake radical changes in how they operate) or face gradual, terminal decline. Attempting to cross the valley by making adjustments but avoiding fundamental change risks demand or financial resources collapsing before the company has reinvented itself. The art, therefore, is to make it across the valley of death before the legacy revenues collapse. That is why timing matters.

Legacy players who started their digital transitions earlier enjoy other benefits too: they have substantial knowledge bases, better industry antennae, and are attuned to the pace of the digital news industry.

Defining the competitive set

Interviewees from the companies profiled here were asked who they viewed as competitors. The legacy companies clearly saw the clean sheet players in this report as competitors. The clean sheet players' attention, however, was focused elsewhere. Notably, they do not see themselves as competing against other providers of journalism, but rather any alternative service or source of information that diverts their target audiences' attention:

> Broadly, I think of every piece of content competing with every other piece of content at all times, and with everything else in your life, for your attention. We don't spend a lot of time thinking about competitors per se. (Interviewee)

> We pay attention most closely to anyone who, like us, is pursuing a social-media-led strategy: the newish and social-media-driven start-ups like BuzzFeed, Business Insider, FiveThirtyEight, Vox, and the Verge, as well as the bloggier sections of the mainstream press like Wonkblog (Washington Post), the Upshot (NYT), and the Guardian, plus any number of more specialist-subject sites. But in a broader sense we also consider every single website and app on a user's phone to be our competition. (Interviewee)

The common pattern underneath successful digital innovation

The stated goal of this chapter, indeed of this book, is to pinpoint common elements underlying these organisations' success with digital news. And a set of common elements has emerged:

- a clear vision that lays out unequivocally what the organisation is trying to do and how this brings benefits to its audiences;
- an equally clear strategy that focuses organisational energies and is embedded in a coherent business model;
- strong leadership from compelling individuals who have both a credible vision and the credibility to sell this vision to a smart workforce and stakeholders;
- enough digital talent, who can enable journalistic, tech, and commercial imperatives to be synthesised;
- a culture that sees digital as an opportunity and understands the importance of tech;
- an organisation that is able to innovate and adapt.

Apart from the melding of journalism, tech, and commercial understanding, these elements are not media-industry-specific. Most are self-evident, if not generic, components of high-performing organisations.

But they do need to be viewed systemically. Their power lies in their combination, in the virtuous circle that is created when all are present and function together. And they may sound prosaic because they have been listed in summary sentences, but each item comprises a bundle of sub-components, each of which benefits the process of innovation. For example, an unequivocal strategic focus involves clear priorities and boundaries, which allows intelligent resource commitment, and brings consistency and agility, and enables the organisations to course correct as necessary.

Further, although prosaic, these elements are also rare. Excellent leadership is rare. A smart vision and strategy are rare, especially a well-executed strategy, and particularly so in highly disrupted markets. A future-focused culture, especially one that has been able to swallow a major technology transition, is also rare.

One last point: these elements are not permanent. Leaders can leave, agile new organisations can become flabby middle-aged ones. A strategy can get caught in its own niche. A strong culture can morph alarmingly quickly into an obstacle if it is tied too tightly to a specific strategic context. And of course, fresh new players will themselves become incumbents over time and innovation will get harder for them.

But what will remain constant is the growth in digital markets. New sectors of the media industry are emerging, and leadership in these is open to any organisation that can innovate in response.

Notes

Chapter 1 Why Are Some Digital News Organisations More Successful than Others?

1 Tony Gallagher, speaking at Media Week at Newswork's Shift 2013 Conference, London, 17 Mar. 2013: http://www.newsworks.org.uk/shift-2013-roving-reports (accessed Nov. 2013).

2 Shane Smith cited in Tim Adams, 'Shane Smith: "I want to build the next CNN with Vice – it's within my grasp"', *Observer,* 24 Mar. 2013: http://www.theguardian.com/media/2013/mar/23/shane-smith-vice-interview (accessed Dec. 2014).

3 Mark Andreessen tweet, 8.15 p.m., 5 Feb. 2014: @pmarca (accessed Feb. 2014).

Chapter 2 The *Guardian* – 'Global, Open, Digital'

1 Alan Rusbridger cited in Ken Auletta, 'Freedom of Information', *The New Yorker,* 7 Oct. 2013: http://www.newyorker.com/magazine/2013/10/07/freedom-of-information (accessed Jan. 2014).

2 Guardian Media Group plc Annual Results, http://www.gmgannualreview2014.com/uploads/overview_press_release.pdf (accessed Mar. 2015).

3 Alan Rusbridger email to staff, cited in Jane Martinson, 'Alan Rusbridger to Stand Down as Editor in Chief', *Guardian,* 10 Dec. 2014: http://www.theguardian.com/media/2014/dec/10/alan-rusbridger-stand-down-guardian-editor-in-chief (accessed Dec. 2014).

4 Tanya Cordrey cited in Vala Afshar, 'The Guardian's Chief Digital Officer on Going "Digital First"', Huffington Post, 16 Mar. 2014: http://www.huffingtonpost.com/vala-afshar/digital-first_b_4975207.html (accessed May 2014).

5 Alan Rusbridger interviewed by Jackie Bennion for PBS *Frontline World,* aired 27 Mar. 2007: http://www.pbs.org/frontlineworld/stories/newswar/guardian (accessed May 2014).

6 Janine Gibson cited in 'Innovation', *New York Times,* 24 Mar. 2014: http://mashable.com/2014/05/16/full-new-york-times-innovation-report (accessed May 2014).

7 Robert Andrews, 'Guardian Hires First Digital Strategy Director to Grow Online Business', Gigaom, 16 Oct. 2012: https://gigaom.com/2012/10/16/

guardian-hires-first-digital-strategy-director-to-grow-online-business (accessed May 2014).

8 Alan Rusbridger cited in Auletta, 'Freedom of Information'.

9 Tanya Cordrey cited in Afshar, 'Guardian's Chief Digital Officer'.

10 Auletta, 'Freedom of Information'.

11 Ken Doctor, 'The Newsonomics of the *Guardian*'s New "Known" Strategy': http://www.niemanlab.org/2014/02/the-newsonomics-of-the-guardians-new-known-strategy (accessed Sept. 2014).

12 Andrew Miller cited in Auletta, 'Freedom of Information'.

13 *Guardian*: www.guardian.com/help/insideguardian/2013/may/24/theguardian-global-domain (accessed May 2014).

14 Auletta, 'Freedom of Information'.

15 Alan Rusbridger interviewed by Bennion, PBS *Frontline World*.

16 Alan Rusbridger cited in Auletta, 'Freedom of Information'.

17 Ibid.

18 Alan Rusbridger interviewed by Bennion, PBS *Frontline World*.

19 Dominic Ponsford, 'Guardian Chief Exec Miller Rejects Metered Paywall Model and Says No More Redundancies Planned', 19 July 2013: http://www.pressgazette.co.uk (accessed Jan. 2014).

20 Alan Rusbridger interviewed by Bennion, PBS *Frontline World*.

21 Michel Rubini, 'The Guardian's Revolution: New Business Model, New Audience, and New Peak Times', Business Wire, 26 Sept. 2012: http://blog.businesswire.com/2012/09/26/the-guardians-revolution-new-business-model-new-audience-and-new-peak-times (accessed Jan. 2014).

22 Ibid.

23 Ibid.

24 Alan Rusbridger's argument to the Scott Trust, cited in Auletta, 'Freedom of Information'.

25 Auletta, 'Freedom of Information'.

26 *The Economist*, 'One Guardian Gone', 21 Jan. 2014: http://www.economist.com/blogs/blighty/2014/01/guardian-sells-trader-media (accessed Jan. 2014).

27 Duncan Robinson, 'Guardian Looks at Compulsory Job Cuts', *Financial Times*, 24 Oct. 2012: http://www.ft.com/intl/cms/s/0/6f03317a-1df9-11e2-ad76-00144feabdc0.html#axzz3PS7VYWiH (accessed Oct. 2012).

28 Dominic Ponsford, 'The Guardian Signs Seven-Figure Deal to Build on "Shared Values" and Provide Branded Content for Unilever', *UK Press Gazette*, 13 Feb 2014: http://www.pressgazette.co.uk/guardian-signs-seven-figure-deal-build-shared-values-provide-branded-content-unilever.

29 Tim de Lisle, 'Can the Guardian Survive?', Intelligent Life, July/Aug. 2012: http://moreintelligentlife.com/content/ideas/tim-de-lisle/can-guardian-survive?page=full (accessed Jan. 2015).

30 Alan Rusbridger cited in Mathew Ingram, 'Why the Guardian is Smart to Bet on Live Events and a Membership Model Instead of Paywalls', Gigaom, 11 Sept. 2014: https://gigaom.com/2014/09/11/why-the-guardian-is-smart-to-bet-on-live-events-and-a-membership-model-instead-of-paywalls (accessed Sept. 2014).

31 Mark Sweney, 'Guardian Media Group Takes 15% Take in Digital Training Company', *Guardian*, 14 Feb. 2014: http://www.theguardian.com/media/2014/feb/14/guardian-media-group-digital-training-decoded (accessed Feb. 2014).

32 De Lisle, 'Can the Guardian Survive?'.

Chapter 3   The *New York Times* – Digitising 'The Grey Lady'

1 Mark Thompson speaking at the Guardian's Activate New York 2013 Summit, 9 Dec. 2013: http://www.theguardian.com/media-network/media-network-blog/video/2013/dec/09/mark-thompson-digital-innovation-new-york-times (accessed June 2014).

2 Ravi Somaiya, 'New York Times Co. Profit Falls Despite Strides in Digital Ads', *New York Times*, 3 Feb. 2015: http://www.nytimes.com/2015/02/04/business/new-york-times-company-q4-earnings.html (accessed Feb. 2015).

3 Trefis Team, 'NYT Earnings: Digital Growth Boosts Revenues Yet Again', Forbes. com, 2 Feb. 2015: http://www.forbes.com/sites/greatspeculations/2015/02/05/nyt-earnings-digital-growth-boosts-revenues-yet-again (accessed Feb. 2015).

4 Nico Hines, 'Meet Mark Thompson, the Winner of Survivor: NYT', Daily Beast, 16 May 2014: http://www.thedailybeast.com/articles/2014/05/16/don-t-mess-with-the-new-york-times-s-mark-thompson.html (accessed Jan. 2015).

5 Joe Pompeo, 'At the "Times", a New Mission Statement', *Capital*, 16 Aug. 2012: http://www.capitalnewyork.com/article/media/2012/08/6448519/times-new-mission-statement (accessed June 2014).

6 Mark Thompson speaking at the FT Digital Media Conference, 25–26 Apr. 2013, London: https://www.youtube.com/watch?v=U55IiVQFdJs (accessed June 2014). The quotation in the immediately preceding subheading is from Mark Thompson cited in Joe Pompeo, 'A Year of Transformation for the *New York Times*', *Capital*, 17 Dec. 2014: http://www.capitalnewyork.com/article/media/2014/12/8558647/year-transformation-emthe-new-york-timesem (accessed Dec. 2014).

7 'The New York Times', Encyclo: http://www.niemanlab.org/encyclo/new-york-times/?=fromembed (accessed June 2014).

8 API stands for Application Program Interface: a set of tools, commands, functions, and protocols that allows programmers to build software for a particular operating system. Publishing APIs means that external parties can build software for the program, and also benefits users, since it means that all programs using an API will have a similar user interface. Twitter, YouTube, and Google Maps are all available, allowing developers to embed these services into their websites.

9 John McDuling, '"The Upshot" is the New York Times' Replacement for Nate Silver's FiveThirtyEight', Quartz, 10 Mar. 2014: http://qz.com/185922/the-upshot-is-the-new-york-times-replacement-for-nate-silvers-fivethirtyeight/ (accessed June 2014).

10 Eric Blattberg, 'Inside the New York Times' Video Strategy', Digiday, 30 Oct. 2014: http://digiday.com/publishers/inside-new-york-times-video-strategy (accessed Jan. 2015).

11 Ibid.

12 Margaret Sullivan, 'A Paper Boat Navigating a Digital Sea', New York Times, 14 June 2014: http:/nyti.ms/1qdGtuJ (accessed June 2014).

13 Patricia Laya and Gerry Smith, 'Billionaire Carlos Slim Doubles Holding in New York Times', Bloomberg, 14 Jan. 2015: http://www.bloomberg.com/news/2015-01-14/carlos-slim-doubles-new-york-times-stake-by-exercising-options.html (accessed Jan. 2015).

14 Ken Doctor, 'The New York Times' Financials Show the Transition to Digital Accelerating', Nieman Lab, 30 Oct. 2014: http://www.niemanlab.org/2014/10/ken-doctor-the-new-york-times-financials-show-a-digital-transition-speeding-up (accessed Oct. 2014).

15 Ken Doctor, 'The Newsonomics of New Cutbacks at the New York Times', Nieman Lab, 1 Oct. 2014: http://www.niemanlab.org/2014/10/the-newsonomics-of-new-cutbacks-at-the-new-york-times (accessed Oct. 2014).

16 Andrew Beaujon, 'NYT Plans Buyouts, Layoffs if Necessary, to Cut 100 Newsroom Staffers', Poynter, 1 Oct. 2014: http://www.poynter.org/news/mediawire/272323/nyt-plans-buyouts-layoffs-if-necessary-to-cut-100-newsroom-staffers (accessed Oct. 2014).

17 Jeff John Roberts, 'The New York Times CEO Calls Digital Pay Model "Most Successful" Decision in Years', Gigaom, 20 May 2014: https://gigaom.com/2013/05/20/new-york-times-ceo-calls-digital-pay-model-most-successful-decision-in-years (accessed May 2014).

18 Ken Doctor, 'The Newsonomics of the New York Times Paywalls 2.0', Nieman Lab, 21 Nov. 2013: http://newsonomics.com/the-newsonomics-of-the-new-york-times-paywalls-2-0 (accessed June 2014).

19 Dean Baquet cited in Margaret Sullivan, 'Dean Baquet's "Charting the Future" Note to Times Staff', New York Times, 6 Jan. 2015: http://publiceditor.blogs.nytimes.com/2015/01/06/dean-baquets-charting-the-future-note-to-times-staff (accessed Jan. 2015).

20 Ibid.

21 Frederic Filloux, 'The New York Times' KPIs', Monday Note, 25 May 2014: http://www.mondaynote.com/2014/05/25/the-new-york-times-kpis (accessed Dec. 2014).

22 Ibid.

23 'The New York Times has sold its soul for a handful of beans': Tom Foremski, 'Here's Why "Native Ads" are a Very Bad Idea … So Why is the NYTimes So Clueless?', ZDNet, 9 Jan. 2014: http://www.zdnet.com/article/heres-why-native-ads-are-a-very-bad-idea-so-why-is-the-nytimes-so-clueless (accessed June 2014).

24 Joe Pompeo, 'Going Native at the *Times*', *Capital*, 29 Sept. 2014: http://www.capitalnewyork.com/article/media/2014/09/8553419/going-native-emtimesem?top-featured-1# (accessed Nov. 2014).

25 Ibid.

26 Lucia Moses, 'Inside T Brand Studio, The New York Times' Native Ad Unit', Digiday, 2 December 2014: http://digiday.com/publishers/new-york-times-native-ad-unit/ (accessed 5 Jan. 2015).

27 Joe Lazauskas, 'How the New York Times Learned to Love Native Advertising', *Content Strategy*, 30 Oct. 2014: http://contently.com/strategist/2014/10/30/to-make-this-work-you-have-got-to-compete-with-editorial-inside-the-nyts-native-ad-journey (accessed Jan. 2015).

28 Tessa Wegert, 'The New York Times Takes Native Advertising to the Next Level with Cole Haan', *Content Strategy*, 10 Oct. 2014: http://contently.com/strategist/2014/10/10/the-new-york-times-takes-native-advertising-to-the-next-level-with-cole-haan (accessed Jan. 2015).

29 Michael Sebastian, 'New York Times Considering New Print Sections, Wants More Native Ads on Mobile', *Advertising Age*, 9 Dec. 2014: http://adage.com/article/media/york-times-bets-native-ads-drive-mobile-ad-revenue/296148 (accessed Jan. 2015).

30 Frederic Filloux, 'Time to Rethink the Newspaper. Seriously', Monday Note, 18 May 2015: http: //mondaynote.com/2014/05/18/time-to-rethink-the-newspaper-seriously (accessed May 2015).

31 Ken Doctor, 'New Numbers from the New York Times: A Gold Star for Managing the Digital Transition', Nieman Journalism Lab, 24 Apr. 2014: http://www.niemanlab.org/2014/04/new-numbers-from-the-new-york-times-a-gold-star-for-managing-the-digital-transition/ (accessed Apr. 2014).

32 *New York Times*, 'Innovation', 24 Mar. 2014: http://mashable.com/2014/05/16/full-new-york-times-innovation-report.

33 Filloux, 'Time to Rethink'.

34 *New York Times*, 'Innovation', 6.

35 Ibid. 7.

36 Michael Moritz, 'What the New York Times Could Have Been', LinkedIn, 20 May 2014: https://www.linkedin.com/pulse/20140520010542-25760-a-south-african-entrepreneur-beats-the-new-york-times-at-its-own-game (accessed Sept. 2014).

37 *New York Times*, 'Innovation', 78.

38 Ibid.

39 Ibid.

40 Ibid. 89.

41 Caroline O'Donovan, 'Q&A: Amy O'Leary on Eight Years of Navigating Digital Culture Change at the New York Times', Nieman Lab, 14 Jan. 2015: http://www.niemanlab.org/2015/01/qa-amy-oleary-on-eight-years-of-navigating-digital-culture-change-at-the-new-york-times (accessed Jan. 2015).

42 Andrew Beaujon, 'NYT Names Arthur Gregg Sulzberger an Editor in Charge of Strategy', Poynter, 14 July 2014: http://www.poynter.org/news/mediawire/258820/nyt-puts-arthur-gregg-sulzberger-in-charge-of-strategy/ (accessed Jan. 2015).

43 Joe Pompeo, 'Times Firms Up Digital Leadership with Kinsey Wilson', *Capital*, 25 Nov. 2014: http://www.capitalnewyork.com/article/media/2014/11/8557365/emtimesem-firms-digital-leadership-kinsey-wilson (accessed Jan. 2015).

44 Caroline O'Donovan, 'Q&A: Amy O'Leary'.

45 Dean Baquet cited in Sullivan, 'Dean Baquet's "Charting the Future" Note'.

46 Alex MacCullum cited in Matthew Ingram, 'News Flash for the NYT: You and BuzzFeed aren't that Different', Gigaom, 15 Jan. 2015: https://gigaom.com/2015/01/14/news-flash-for-the-nyt-you-and-buzzfeed-arent-that-different (accessed Jan. 2015).

47 Mathew Ingram, 'At Long Last, the New York Times is Thinking about Digital First', Gigaom, 19 Feb. 2015, https://gigaom.com/2015/02/19/at-long-last-the-new-york-times-is-thinking-about-digital-first (accessed Feb. 2015).

48 Sullivan, 'Paper Boat'.

Chapter 4 Quartz – What Would *The Economist* Look Like if it had Been Born in 2012?

1 Zachary Seward, interviewed in Alastair Reed, 'The Death of the Homepage, or Another Evolution', podcast from journalism.co.uk., 30 May 2014: https://www.journalism.co.uk/podcast/the-death-of-the-homepage-or-another-evolution-/s399/a556939 (accessed Aug. 2014).

2 Frederic Filloux, 'The Quartz Way (1)', Monday Note, 6 Oct. 2013: http://www.mondaynote.com/2013/10/06/the-quartz-way-1 (accessed Aug. 2014).

3 Filloux, 'Quartz Way (1)'.

4 Ibid.

5 Data from Quartz, 18 Nov. 2014.

6 Kevin Delaney cited in Roger Yu, 'Quartz Seeks Wider Audience as Competition Stiffens', *USA Today*, 23 June 2014: http://www.usatoday.com/story/money/business/2014/06/23/quartz-competes-in-data-journalism/10606473 (accessed Oct. 2014).

7 Data from Quartz, 18 Nov. 2014.

8 Justin Smith cited in Jeremy W. Peters, 'Web Focus Helps Revitalize The Atlantic', *New York Times*, 12 Dec. 2010: http://www.nytimes.com/2010/12/13/business/media/13atlantic.html?pagewanted=all&_r=0 (accessed Aug. 2014).

9 Frederic Filloux, 'The Quartz Way (2)', Monday Note, 13 Oct. 2013: http://www.mondaynote.com/2013/10/06/the-quartz-way-2 (accessed Aug. 2014).

10 Peters, 'Web Focus Helps Revitalize'.

11 Filloux, 'Quartz Way (2)'.

12 Jay Lauf cited in Jasper Jackson, 'Quartz and The Economist on What Makes a Good Media Business Today and Tomorrow', The Media Briefing, 20 Nov. 2014: http://www.themediabriefing.com/article/rossi-lauf-quartz-economist-media-company-now-future (accessed Dec. 2014).

13 Society of American Business Editors and Writers, 2013 Winners List: http://sabew.org/2014/02/2013-bib-winners-list (accessed Dec. 2014).

14 Jay Lauf cited in Jackson, 'Quartz and The Economist'.

15 Jay Lauf cited in Kevin Delaney, 'NewsRewired 2013: Three Things Driving QZ.com's Journalism', SUW Charman Anderson, 20 Sept. 2013: http:charman-anderson.com/2013/newsrewired-2013-three-things-driving-qz-coms-journalism (accessed Aug. 2014).

16 Richard Edelman, 'Quartz, the Quality Play', 6 a.m., 25 Apr. 2014: http://www.Edelman.com/p/6-a-m/quartz-the-quality-play (accessed Dec. 2014).

17 Jay Lauf cited in Kevin, 'NewsRewired 2013'.

18 Josh Sternberg, 'Kevin Delaney Tinkers with Media at Quartz', Digiday, 15 Nov. 2013: http://digiday.com/publishers/sonobi-kevin-delaney-quartz (accessed Nov. 2014).

19 Kevin Delaney cited in Yu, 'Quartz Seeks Wider Audience'.

20 Edelman, 'Quartz, the Quality Play'.

21 Kevin Delaney cited in Ken Doctor, 'The Newsonomics of Quartz, 19 Months In', Nieman Lab, 1 May 2014: http://niemanlab.org/2014/05/the-newsonomics-of-quartz-19-months-in (accessed June 2014).

22 Jeremy Littau cited in Yu, 'Quartz Seeks Wider Audience'.

23 Max Nisen, 'What the Top US Engineering Schools have in Common with Hogwarts', Quartz, 3 Aug. 2014: http://qz.com/243031/what-the-countrys-top-engineering-schools-have-in-common-with-hogwarts (accessed Jan. 2015).

24 Kevin Delaney cited in Yu, 'Quartz Seeks Wider Audience'.

25 Kevin Delaney cited in Doctor, 'Newsonomics of Quartz, 19 Months In'.

26 Ben Cardew, 'Data Nuggets Drive Quartz's News Agenda Which Digs Deep into Business', Guardian, 30 May 2014: http://www.theguardian.com/media/2014/mar/30/quartz-mobile-first-business-data-nuggets?CMP=ema_546 (accessed May 2014).

27 Randy Dahlke, 'How Did Quartz Get 5 Million Unique Visitors a Month in Just 18 Months? Native Ads', http://nativemobile.com/quartz-get-5-million-unique-visitors-month-just-18-months-native-ads-7482 (accessed Nov. 2014).

28 Christopher Mims, '59 Percent of America's Tuna Isn't Actually Tuna', http://qz.com/55699/59-percent-of-americas-tuna-isnt-actually-tuna (accessed Aug. 2014).

29 Dahlke, 'How Did Quartz Get 5 Million Unique Visitors?'.

30 Kevin Delaney cited in Edelman, 'Quartz, the Quality Play'.

31 Jay Lauf cited in Edelman, 'Quartz, the Quality Play'.

32 Roberto A. Ferdman, 'Which US States Tip the Most as Shown by Millions of Square Transactions', Quartz, 21 Mar. 2014: http://qz.com/189458/the-united-states-of-tipping (accessed Aug. 2014).

33 Zachary Seward, 'Quartz Has a New Look – and for the First Time, a Homepage', Quartz, 24 Aug. 2014: http://qz.com/246831/quartz-has-a-new-look-and-for-the-first-time-a-homepage (accessed Aug. 2014).

34 Zachary Seward, interviewed by Alistair Reid, ibid.

35 Zachary Seward, 'Quartz Has a New Look'.

36 Henry Taylor, 'How to Build a Successful Newsletter: Advice from Quartz', The Media Briefing, 26 June 2014: http://www.themediabriefing.com/article/quartz-newsletters-advice-simon-davies-daily-brief (accessed Sept. 2014).

37 Gideon Litchfield, Quartz Weekend Brief, 27 Dec. 2014.

38 Kevin Delaney cited in Doctor, 'Newsonomics of Quartz, 19 Months In'.

39 Filloux, 'Quartz Way (1)'.

40 Sam Kirkland, 'AJC Reorganizes Newsroom for Digital with Topic Teams Inspired by Quartz's Obsessions', Poynter, 18 June 2014: http://www.poynter.org/media-innovation/media-lab/256022/ajcs-digital-reorganization-part-1-topic-teams-inspired-by-quartzs-obsessions (accessed Nov. 2014).

41 Yu, 'Quartz Seeks Wider Audience'.

42 Cardew, 'Data Nuggets Drive Quartz's News Agenda'.

43 Yu, 'Quartz Seeks Wider Audience'.

44 Kevin, 'NewsRewired 2013: Three Things Driving QZ.com's Journalism'.

45 David Yanofsky, 'How to Turn Everyone in Your Newsroom into a Graphics Editor', Nieman Lab, 30 July 2013: http://www.niemanlab.org/2013/07/how-to-turn-everyone-in-your-newsroom-into-a-graphics-editor/. (accessed 13 August 2014).

46 Kevin Delaney cited in Edelman, 'Quartz, the Quality Play'.

47 Kevin Delaney cited in Doctor, 'Newsonomics of Quartz, 19 Months In'.

48 Jackson, 'Quartz and The Economist'.
49 Seward, 'Quartz Has a New Look'.
50 Jay Lauf cited in Josh Sternberg, 'Is Quartz the Very Model of Modern Publisher?', Digiday, 30 May 2013: http://digiday.com/publishers/is-quartz-the-very-model-of-a-modern-publisher (accessed Dec. 2014).
51 Kevin Delaney cited in Doctor, 'Newsonomics of Quartz, 19 Months In'.
52 Jay Lauf, cited in Kevin, 'NewsRewired 2013: Three Things Driving QZ.com's Journalism'.
53 Yu, 'Quartz Seeks Wider Audience'.

Chapter 5   BuzzFeed – Making Life More Interesting for the Hundreds of Millions Bored at Work

1 Jonah Peretti speaking at 'Kara Swisher, Jonah Peretti, Shane Smith, and David Carron New and Old Media', Vanity Fair's New Establishment Summit, 28 Oct. 2014: http://video.vanityfair.com/watch/the-new-establishment-summit-kara-swisher-jonah-peretti-shane-smith-david-carr-new-and-old-media (accessed Nov. 2014).
2 Jonah Peretti cited in Cdixonblog, 'BuzzFeed's Strategy', 24 July 2012: http://cdixon.org/2012/07/24/buzzfeeds-strategy (accessed Aug. 2014).
3 http://www.crunchbase.com/organization/buzzfeed (accessed Nov. 2014).
4 Peter Kafka, 'BuzzFeed's New Strategy: Fishing for Eyeballs in Other People's Streams', Recode, 16 Mar. 2015: http://recode.net/2015/03/16/buzzfeeds-new-strategy-fishing-for-eyeballs-in-other-peoples-streams (accessed Mar. 2015).
5 'BuzzFeed Changes European Head', Euro2Day, 19 Mar. 2015: http://www.euro2day.gr/ftcom_en/article-ft-en/1314039/buzzfeed-changes-european-head.html, (accessed Mar. 2015).
6 Statistics from BuzzFeed by email, 13 Jan. and 17 Nov. 2015.
7 Will Oremus, 'BuzzFeed Plagiarism, Deleted Posts: Jonah Peretti Explains', Slate, Aug. 2014: http://slate.com/articles/technology/2014/08 (accessed Oct. 2014).
8 Jonah Peretti interviewed on Nieman Lab Riptide: http://www.niemanlab.org/riptide/person/jonah-peretti (accessed Oct. 2014).
9 'Nike ID Sweatshop E-mail Controversy': http://knowyourmeme.com/memes/events/nike-id-sweatshop-e-mail-controversy#fn24 (accessed Jan. 2015) (author and date data not available).
10 Jonah Peretti cited in Cdixonblog, 'BuzzFeed's Strategy'.
11 Jonah Peretti interviewed by Chris Dixon for the a16z podcast, 'For BuzzFeed Sharing is the Metric that Matters', 18 Sept. 2014: https://soundcloud.com/a16z/a16z-podcast-sharing-is-the-metric-that-matters-building-buzzfeed-for-a-socialmobile-world (accessed Jan. 2015).
12 Alyson Shontell, 'Here's What Happened to BuzzFeed's Facebook Traffic Which Seems to be Tanking', Business Insider, 12 June 2014: http://www.businessinsider.com/how-quizzes-affected-buzzfeeds-facebook-traffic-in-2014-2014-6?IR=T (accessed Aug. 2014).
13 Jonah Peretti cited in Peter Kafka, 'BuzzFeed's Growth Czar is Now its Publisher', Recode, 14 Oct. 2014: http://recode.net/2014/10/14/buzzfeeds-growth-czar-is-now-its-publisher (accessed Oct. 2014).

14 Jonah Peretti cited in Cdixonblog, 'BuzzFeed's Strategy'.

15 Ibid.

16 Jonah Peretti cited in Kadhim Shubber, 'BuzzFeed's Jonah Peretti on Balancing Investigative Journalism with Cute Kittens', Wired Blog, 16 Oct. 2013: http://www.wired.co.uk/news/archive/2013-10/16/buzzfeed-jonah-peretti (accessed May 2014).

17 Jonah Peretti cited in Cdixonblog, 'BuzzFeed's Strategy'.

18 Jonah Peretti interviewed by Chris Dixon for the a16z podcast.

19 Jonah Peretti interviewed on Nieman Lab Riptide.

20 Jonah Peretti cited in Cdixonblog, 'BuzzFeed's Strategy'.

21 Ibid.

22 Ibid.

23 BuzzFeed press release, 'BuzzFeed Announces Major Expansion across All Business Lines', 11 Aug. 2014: http://www.buzzfeed.com/buzzfeedpress/buzzfeed-announces-major-expansion-across-all-business-lines#.aiEwbmWw0b (accessed Aug. 2014).

24 Ben Smith, 'Why BuzzFeed Doesn't Do Clickbait', 6 Nov. 2014: http://www.buzzfeed.com/bensmith/why-buzzfeed-doesnt-do-clickbait#.swqPMz1PqM (accessed Jan. 2015).

25 Jeff Bercovici, 'BuzzFeed is Officially a Case Study in Media Industry Disruption', Forbes.com, 7 July 2014: http://www.forbes.com/sites/jeff/2014/07/07/buzzfeed-is-officially-a-case-study-in-media-industry-disruption (accessed July 2014).

26 BuzzFeed press release, 'BuzzFeed Announces Major Expansion'.

27 Andrew Beaujon, 'How Much Does BuzzFeed Write About Cats, Anyway?', 19 May 2014: http://www.poynter.org/news/mediawire/252706/how-much-does-buzzfeed-write-about-cats-anyway (accessed May 2014).

28 Jonah Peretti interviewed by Chris Dixon for the a16z podcast.

29 Jonah Peretti interviewed in Niklas Wirminghaus, 'LOL, WIN, OMG: Founder Jonah Peretti about BuzzFeed's Recipe for Success', Venture Village, 3 Mar. 2014: http://venturevillage.eu/jonah-peretti-interview (accessed Jan. 2015).

30 BuzzFeed press release, 'BuzzFeed Announces Major Expansion'.

31 Lisa O'Carroll, 'BuzzFeed Moves into Profit', Guardian, 5 Sept. 2013: http://www.theguardian.com/media/2013/sep/05/buzzfeed-listicle-profit-jonah-peretti (accessed May 2014).

32 Jonah Peretti, Linkedin post, 'Memo to the BuzzFeed Team': https://www.linkedin.com/today/post/article/20130904212907-1799428-memo-to-the-buzzfeed-team (accessed May 2014).

33 Carmel Deamicis, 'Jonah Peretti: Both Time and BuzzFeed Grew by Creating Irresistible Lists', Pando Daily, 6 Mar. 2014: http://pando.com/2014/03/06/jonah-peretti-both-time-and-buzzfeed-grew-by-creating-irresistible-lists (accessed Mar. 2014).

34 Jonah Peretti, Linkedin post, 'Memo'.

35 Alyson Shontell, 'Inside BuzzFeed: The Story of How Jonah Peretti Built the Web's Most Beloved New Media Brand', Business Insider, 11 Dec. 2012: http://www.businessinsider.com/buzzfeed-jonah-peretti-interview-2012-12?IR=T (accessed Aug. 2014).

36 Catalina Albeanu, 'BuzzFeed Appoints New Senior Writer', Journalism.co.uk, 4 Dec. 2014: https://www.journalism.co.uk/news/buzzfeed-uk-appoints-new-senior-writer-plans-to-expand-with-beat-structure-/s2/a563386/ (accessed Jan. 2015).

37 Shontell, 'Inside BuzzFeed'.

38 Jonah Peretti interviewed on Nieman Lab Riptide.

39 Ben Smith cited in Megan Garber, 'Breaking News is Broken: Could BuzzFeed be the One to Fix it?, Atlantic.com, 25 Apr. 2013: http://www.theatlantic.com/technology/archive/2013/04/breaking-news-is-broken-could-buzzfeed-be-the-one-to-fix-it/275310 (accessed May 2014).

40 Abigail Edge, 'BuzzFeed: Why Publishers Should Avoid Siloing Content', Journalism.co.uk, 16 Oct. 2014: https://www.journalism.co.uk/news/buzzfeed-why-news-outlets-should-avoid-siloing-content/s2/a562837 (accessed Oct. 2014).

41 Oremus, 'BuzzFeed Plagiarism'.

42 Ibid.

43 BuzzFeed press release, 'BuzzFeed Announces Major Expansion'.

44 Michael Sebastian, 'Q&A: Greg Coleman's Programmatic Plans for BuzzFeed', *Advertising Age*, 6 Aug. 2014: http://adage.com/article/media/q-a-buzzfeed-president-greg-coleman/294487 (accessed Aug. 2014).

45 BuzzFeed press release, 'BuzzFeed Announces Major Expansion'.

46 Jonah Peretti interviewed by Chris Dixon for the a16z podcast.

47 Eric Blattberg, 'The Secret to BuzzFeed's Video Success: Data', Digiday, 24 Sept. 2014: http://digiday.com/publishers/inside-buzzfeed-video (accessed Sept. 2014).

48 Eddie Scarry, 'BuzzFeed Brews: "It's like a first date"', Fishbowl DC, 6 Feb. 2013: http://www.mediabistro.com/fishbowldc/buzzfeed-brews-marco-rubio-ben-smith-john-stanton_b95711 (accessed May 2014).

49 Jonah Peretti interviewed by Chris Dixon for the a16z podcast.

50 Jonah Peretti interviewed on Nieman Lab Riptide.

51 Bercovici, 'BuzzFeed Case Study in Disruption'.

52 Jonah Peretti interviewed by Chris Dixon for the a16z podcast.

53 Deamicis, 'Jonah Peretti: Both Time and BuzzFeed'.

54 Jonah Peretti interviewed by Chris Dixon for the a16z podcast.

55 Jonah Peretti cited in Shubber, 'Balancing Investigative Journalism with Cute Kittens'.

56 Sebastian, 'Q&A: Greg Coleman's Plans'.

57 Jonah Peretti, Linkedin post, 'Memo'.

58 Ibid.

59 Ibid.

60 Ibid.

61 Ibid.

Chapter 6   Vice Media – 'We are the Changing of the Guard'

1 Shane Smith interviewed by Miguel Helft for *Fortune Magazine*, 14 Oct. 2013, http://fortune.com/2013/10/14/vice-ceo-on-old-media-they-can-go-to-hell-quite-frankly (accessed Oct. 2014).

2 Shane Smith cited in Matthew Garrahan, 'Lunch with the FT: Shane Smith', *Financial Times*, 28 Dec. 2012, http://www.ft.com/intl/cms/s/2/61c51d64-4a9c-11e2-968a-00144feab49a.html#axzz3KBNwBejz (accessed Nov. 2014).

3 http://www.vice.com (accessed Jan. 2015).

4 Shane Smith interviewed by Miguel Helft for *Fortune*.

5 Ibid.

6 Edwin Smith, 'How $1.4bn Vice is Changing the Media Guard', *Telegraph*, 16 Nov. 2013: uk.finance.yahoo.com/news/1-4bn-vice-changing-media-160401079. html (accessed Dec. 2014).

7 http://www.crunchbase.com/organization/vice (accessed Nov. 2014).

8 http://www.forbes.com/sites/pascalemmanuelgobry/2014/03/31/vice-media-ipo (accessed Nov. 2014).

9 Garrahan, 'Lunch with the FT: Shane Smith'.

10 Shane Smith cited in Paul Sandie, 'Vice Media Uses Gonzo Sensibility to Win Online', reuters.com, 4 Nov. 2013: http://www.reuters.com/article/2013/11/04/us-vicemedia-idUSBRE9A30R620131104 (accessed Dec. 2014).

11 Matthew Garrahan, '21st Century Fox Takes Stake in "Gonzo" Vice, *Financial Times*, 16 Aug. 2013: http://www.ft.com/intl/cms/s/2/e2db3cc4-0664-11e3-9bd9-00144feab7de.html#axzz3KBNwBejz (accessed Nov. 2014).

12 Shane Smith cited in Sandie, Vice Media Uses Gonzo Sensibility'.

13 Shane Smith cited in Tim Adams, 'Shane Smith: "I want to build the Next CNN with Vice – It's Within My Grasp"', *Observer*, 24 Mar. 2013: http://www. theguardian.com/media/2013/mar/23/shane-smith-vice-interview (accessed Dec. 2014).

14 Source: Vice, 24 June 2015.

15 Edwin Smith, 'How $1.4bn Vice is Changing the Media Guard'.

16 Garrahan, 'Lunch with the FT: Shane Smith'.

17 Mark Coles, 'Shane Smith', BBC Radio 4 profile, first broadcast 21 Sept. 2014: http://www.bbc.co.uk/programmes/b04hmdks (accessed Sept. 2014).

18 Garrahan, 'Lunch with the FT: Shane Smith'.

19 Matthew Garrahan, 'Shane Smith, the Hard-Partying Mogul Who has Won Over the Millennials', *Financial Times*, 13 June 2014: http://www.ft.com/intl/cms/s/2/ad90e5d2-f227-11e3-9015-00144feabdc0.html (accessed Nov. 2014).

20 Rebecca Lieb cited in Scott Martin, 'Vice Media Cranks Up News Operations', usatoday.com, 16 Dec. 2013: http://www.usatoday.com/story/tech/2013/12/16/vice-media-cranks-up-news-operations/3699639 (accessed Dec. 2014).

21 Shane Smith cited in Adams, 'Shane Smith: Next CNN'.

22 Shane Smith, speaking at *Vanity Fair*'s New Establishment Summit.

23 Ibid.

24 Ibid.

25 Ibid.

26 Caption to blogged photo published in connection with McAfee story, cited in Adams, 'Shane Smith: Next CNN'.

27 Shane Smith cited in Adams, 'Shane Smith: Next CNN'.

28 Ibid.

29 Garrahan, 'Shane Smith, the Hard-Partying Mogul'.

30 Mat Honan, 'How Trusting in Vice Led to John McAfee's Downfall', 12 June 2012: http://www.wired.com/2012/12/how-vice-got-john-mcafee-caught (accessed Dec. 2014).

31 http://www.vice.com/read/our-official-statement-on-the-mcafee-saga (accessed Dec. 2014).

32 Shane Smith cited in Marisa Guthrie, 'Vice CEO Shane Smith: Asking Dennis Rodman about Geopolitics is a Cheap Shot', *Hollywood Reporter*, 14 June 2013 (http://www.hollywoodreporter.com/live-feed/vice-ceo-shane-smith-asking-569182 (accessed Dec. 2013).

33 Garrahan, 'Lunch with the FT: Shane Smith'.

34 Shane Smith, speaking at *Vanity Fair*'s New Establishment Summit.

35 Robert Nolan, 'Vice's North Korea Gambit More Jackass than Journalism', *US News and World Report*, 28 Feb. 2013: http://www.usnews.com/opinion/blogs/world-report/2013/02/28/vices-dennis-rodman-north-korea-gambit-only-about-publicity (accessed Oct. 2014).

36 Shane Smith interviewed by Miguel Helft for *Fortune*.

37 Shane Smith, speaking at *Vanity Fair*'s New Establishment Summit.

38 Shane Smith interviewed by Miguel Helft for *Fortune*.

39 Jon Swaine, 'Vice's Shane Smith: "Young People are Angry and Leaving TV in Droves"', *Guardian*, 2 Mar. 2014: http://www.theguardian.com/media/2014/mar/02/vice-media-shane-smith-north-korea (accessed Dec. 2014).

40 Tom Freston interviewed by Mark Coles, 'Shane Smith', BBC Radio 4 profile.

41 Shane Smith cited in Guthrie, 'Vice CEO Shane Smith'.

42 Shane Smith interviewed by Miguel Helft for *Fortune*.

43 Ibid.

44 Shane Smith, speaking at *Vanity Fair*'s New Establishment Summit.

45 Hamilton Nolan, 'Working at Vice Media is Not as Cool as it Seems', Gawker.com, 30 May 2014: http://gawker.com/working-at-vice-media-is-not-as-cool-as-it-seems-1579711577 (accessed Nov. 2014).

46 Peter Sterne, 'Former Vice Media Editor Says Company Killed Stories Over "Brand Partner" Concerns', *Capital New York*, 2 Oct. 2014: http://www.capitalnewyork.com/article/media/2014/10/8553826/former-vice-media-editor-says-company-killed-stories-over-brand-partner (accessed Oct. 2014).

47 Shane Smith, speaking at *Vanity Fair*'s New Establishment Summit.

48 Edwin Smith, 'How $1.4bn Vice is Changing the Media Guard'.

49 Shane Smith cited ibid.

50 Shane Smith interviewed by Miguel Helft for *Fortune*.

51 Garrahan, '21st Century Fox'.

Chapter 7   Conclusions – So Why *Are* Some Digital News Organisations More Successful?

1 Exchange between Shane Smith and Jonah Peretti, *Vanity Fair*'s New Establishment Summit.

2 Ezra Klein cited in Leslie Kaufman, 'Vox Takes Melding of Journalism and Technology to a New Level', *New York Times*, 6 Apr. 2014, http://www.nytimes.com/2014/04/07/business/media/voxcom-takes-melding-of-journalism-and-technology-to-next-level.html (accessed Mar. 2014).

3 C. W. Anderson, 'How Journalists' Self-Concepts Hindered their Adaptation to a Digital World', Nieman Lab, 17 Jan. 2013: http://www.niemanlab.org/2013/01/c-w-anderson-how-journalists-self-concepts-hindered-their-adaptation-to-a-digital-world/ (accessed Aug. 2014).

4 Molly Graham cited in '80 Percent of Your Culture is Your Founder', First Round: http://firstround.com/article/80-of-Your-Culture-is-Your-Founder (accessed Aug. 2014).

5 Robinson Meyer, 'The New York Times' Most Popular Story of 2013 was Not an Article', The Atlantic, 17 Jan. 2014: http://www.theatlantic.com/technology/archive/2014/01/-em-the-new-york-times-em-most-popular-story-of-2013-was-not-an-article/283167 (accessed Sept. 2014).

6 Paul Williams, 'Learning the Right Lessons from Digital News Leaders', Medium.com, 6 Oct. 2014: https://medium.com/@paujwill/learning-the-right-lessons-from-digital-news-leaders-bb5107183e12 (accessed Oct. 2014).

7 Clay Shirky blog, 'Newspapers and Thinking the Unthinkable', posted Mar. 2009, http://www.shirky.com/weblog/2009/03/newspapers-and-thinking-the-unthinkable (accessed Feb. 2012).

8 Ravi Somaiya, 'How Facebook is Changing the Way its Users Consume Journalism', New York Times, 26 Oct. 2014: http://www.nytimes.com/2014/10/27/business/media/how-facebook-is-changing-the-way-its-users-consume-journalism.html (accessed Oct. 2014).

9 Williams, 'Learning the Right Lessons'.

10 Somaiya, 'How Facebook is Changing the Way'.

11 Shailesh Prakash cited in Jasper Jackson, 'WaPo CIO on Making the Most of New Technology: "It's not a science, it's an art"', The Media Briefing, 11 July 2014: themediabriefing.com/article/wapo-cto-on-being-prepared-for-new-tech-it-s-not-a-science-it-s-an-art (accessed July 2014).

12 Alan Rusbridger's speech at Columbia Journalism School in acceptance of Columbia University Journalism Award, 21 May 2014: https://www.youtube.com/watch?v=h_tQKIgZ7E8 (accessed July 2014).

13 Clark Gilbert cited in Paul Beebe, 'Deseret News' Transformation to a Worldwide Information Business: What Can your Business Learn from its Strategy?', Utah Business, 1 Mar. 2014: http://www.thefreelibrary.com/Deseret+news%27+transformation+to+a+worldwide+information+business%3A...-a0366460497.

14 Ken Doctor, 'The Newsonomonics of the New York Times' Innovators' Dilemma', Nieman Lab, 22 May 2014, http://www.niemanlab.org/2014/05/the-newsonomics-of-the-new-york-times-innovators-dilemmas/ (accessed May 2014).

15 Andrew Grove and Robert Burgelman, Strategic Dynamics: Three Key Themes, Stanford Graduate School Research paper, No, 2096 (Stanford, CA, 1 Mar. 2012).

Interviewees

I am indebted to the many individuals who generously made themselves available for interviews, put me in contact with peers and provided research data for this project. Inside the case study organisations these include:

- At the *Guardian*: Sheila Fitzsimmons, Janine Gibson, Aron Pilhofer, Alan Rusbridger, Anthony Sullivan
- At the *New York Times*: Will Bardeen, Mark Thompson
- At Quartz: Simon Davies, Bobby Ghosh, Gideon Lichfield, Emily Passer
- At BuzzFeed: Will Hayward, Ben Smith, Alice Suh
- At Vice: Jade Hooker, Matt O'Mara, Kevin Sutcliffe

I am also grateful to a number of expert interviewees who also provided valuable input. These include:

- Emily Bell (Columbia University Graduate School of Journalism)
- Lou Ferrara (Associated Press)
- Andrew Golis (This)
- Jimmy Maymann (Huffington Post)
- Jeff Sonderman (American Press Institute)
- Tom Standage (*The Economist*)
- Daniel Williamson (TheMediaBriefing)

Acknowledgements

This research has been made possible by support from the Reuters Institute for the Study of Journalism at the University of Oxford. I would like to thank David Levy for his continued engagement with this research project and many valuable inputs, Alex Reid for her expert support during the publishing process, and the expert readers and members of the Editorial Committee for their constructive feedback and input.

At the *Guardian*, Natalie Ray, and at the *New York Times*, Mary Ellen LaManna, were tremendously helpful fixing up interviews.

On a personal note, Elizabeth Hennessy, Elisabeth Kaland, Anke and Brian Ma Siy, Barbara Mellor, Jill Shankleman, and Fran Synge all contributed greatly and I am grateful for their support.

My biggest thanks, of course, go to Gebi and Hira Maya for their continued good humour, patience, and interest in a project that did not always follow the course planned. This book is for you.

RISJ/I.B.TAURIS PUBLICATIONS

CHALLENGES

Innovators in Digital News
Lucy Küng
ISBN: 978 1 78453 416 5

Journalism and PR: News Media and Public Relations in the Digital Age
John Lloyd and Laura Toogood
ISBN: 978 1 78453 062 4

Reporting the EU: News, Media and the European Institutions
John Lloyd and Cristina Marconi
ISBN: 978 1 78453 065 5

Women and Journalism
Suzanne Franks
ISBN: 978 1 78076 585 3

Climate Change in the Media: Reporting Risk and Uncertainty
James Painter
ISBN: 978 1 78076 588 4

Transformations in Egyptian Journalism
Naomi Sakr
ISBN: 978 1 78076 589 1

EDITED VOLUMES

Media, Revolution and Politics in Egypt: The Story of an Uprising
Abdalla F. Hassan
ISBN: 978 1 78453 217 8 (HB); 978 1 78453 218 5 (PB)

The Euro Crisis in the Media: Journalistic Coverage of Economic Crisis and European Institutions
Robert G. Picard (ed.)
ISBN: 978 1 78453 059 4 (HB); 978 1 78453 060 0 (PB)

Local Journalism: The Decline of Newspapers and the Rise of Digital Media
Rasmus Kleis Nielsen (ed.)
ISBN: 978 1 78453 320 5 (HB); 978 1 78453 321 2 (PB)

The Ethics of Journalism: Individual, Institutional and Cultural Influences
Wendy N. Wyatt (ed.)
ISBN: 978 1 78076 673 7 (HB); 978 1 78076 674 4 (PB)

Political Journalism in Transition: Western Europe in a Comparative Perspective
Raymond Kuhn and Rasmus Kleis Nielsen (eds)
ISBN: 978 1 78076 677 5 (HB); 978 1 78076 678 2 (PB)

Transparency in Politics and the Media: Accountability and Open Government
Nigel Bowles, James T. Hamilton and David A. L. Levy (eds)
ISBN: 978 1 78076 675 1 (HB); 978 1 78076 676 8 (PB)

Media and Public Shaming: Drawing the Boundaries of Disclosure
Julian Petley (ed.)
ISBN: 978 1 78076 586 0 (HB); 978 1 78076 587 7 (PB)